Social Resilience and State Fragility in Haiti

THE WORLD BANK
Washington, D.C.

ISBN-13: 978-0-8213-7187-9
eISBN: 978-0-8213-7188-6
ISSN: 0253-2123   DOI: 10.1596/978-0-8213-7187-9

Cover photo by Jacob Holdt

Library of Congress Cataloging-in-Publication Data has been requested.

Contents

LIST OF TABLES

LIST OF FIGURES

Preface

Dorte Verner and Willy Egset (task team leaders and the main authors of this report) led the report team. The work was based on the findings of various missions that visited Haiti during 2005, and on additional research undertaken during 2004. The task team includes Stephanie Kuttner, Michael Justesen, Gillette Hall, Dan Erikson (consultant, Inter-American Dialogue), Katherine Bain, Emma Grant, and Franka Braun. The report does not reflect developments since February 17, 2006.

This report is the result of collaboration among several Bank units. Funding for the study was contributed by the Haiti Country Management Unit, the Social Development Department, the Conflict Prevention and Reconstruction Unit, the LICUS/Fragile State Unit, and the PREM Civil Society Group in Latin America. The funding is gratefully acknowledged.

Background papers, notes, and direct input to the report were prepared by Gillette Hall (social protection), Dan Erikson (political situation), Willy Egset and Mark Mattner (urban violence), Michael Justesen and Dorte Verner (youth), Stephanie Kuttner (governance), Dorte Verner (poverty, growth, and labor markets), Katherine Bain, Emma Grant, and Franka Braun (non-state service provision), and Nathalie Lamaute, Gilles Damai, and Willy Egset (rural governance and local institutions). Andrew Crawley edited the report and Vivian Callaghan provided administrative support. The report was produced under the supervision of Caroline Anstey, Director, and McDonald Benjamin, Sector Manager.

The members of the team would like to thank other Bank staff and individuals from outside the Bank for support, guidance, and comments. Special thanks are due to Joelle Dehasse, Senior Country Officer, for her support throughout the process. Several other people helped the team, including Christian Lotz, Per Wam, Antonella Bassani, Estanislao Gacitua-Mario, Garry Charlier, Pierre Werbrouk, Mark Mattner, John Redwood, Mark Schneider (International Crisis Group), Jocelyn McCalla (National Coalition for Haitian Rights), Jim Dobbins (RAND Corporation), and John Horton (Inter-American Development Bank). In Haiti, Nathalie Brisson Lamaute, Gilles Damais, and Dominique Mathon supervised data collection and analysis for some of the background papers under very challenging and sometimes dangerous conditions.

The views expressed in this report are exclusively those of the authors.

Abbreviations and Acronyms

ASEC	Assemblée de la Section Communale	Assembly of the Section Communale
AIDS	Syndrome Immuno-deficitaire acquis	Acquired Immunodeficiency Syndrome
ANAMAH	Association des juges haïtiens	Association of Haitian Judges
APENA	Administration Nationale De Prison	National Penitentiary Administration
CASEC	Le Conseil administratif de la section communale	Administrative Council of the Section Communal
CASER	Conseil d'administration de la section rurale	Board of Directors of the Rural Section
CAMEP	Centrale Autonome Métropolitaine d'Eau Potable	Metropolitan Autonomous Drinking Water Station
CCI/ICF	Cadre de Coopération Interimaire	Interim Cooperation Framework
CID	Le Conseil Interdépartemental	Interdepartmental Council
CIMO	Compagnie d'Intervention et du Maintien d'Ordre	Company for Intervention and the Maintenance of Order
CT	Autoritès locales	Local authorities
DHS	Enquêtes démographiques et de santé	Demographic and Health Surveys
EBCM	Enquête budget-consommation des ménages	Household Budget-Consumption Survey
ECD	Developpement de la petite enfance	Early Childhood Development
ECVH	Enquete sur les Conditions de Vie en Haiti	Inquire into the Living conditions in Haiti
EDH	Electricite d'Haiti	Electricity of Haiti
EMA	Ecole de la Magistrature	School of the Judiciary
EU	Union Européenne	European Union
FAd'H	Anciennes forces armées d'Haïti	Former Armed Forces of Haiti
FAES	Fonds d'Assistance Economique et Sociale	Economic and Social Assistance Funds
FAFO	Institut pour les sciences sociales appliquées	Institute for Applied Social Sciences
G		Haitian gourde (currency unit)
GDP	Produit national brut	Gross domestic product
GIPNH	Groupe d'Intervention de la Police Nationale d'Haiti	Intervention Group of the National Police of Haiti
GNI		Gross national income
HIV/AIDS	Virus Humain D'Immunodéficit (HIV) et syndrome acquis d'immunodéficit (SIDA).	Human Immunodeficiency Virus (HIV) and Acquired Immunodeficiency Syndrome (AIDS)
HLCS	Enquête sur le mode de vie en Haïti	Haiti Living Conditions Survey

HNP	Police Nationale Haïtienne	Haitian National Police
HRW	Surveillance de Droits de l'homme	Human Rights Watch
IACHR	La Commission Inter-Américaine sur des droits de l'homme	Inter-American Commission on Human Rights
ICF	Cadre De Coopération D'Intérim	Interim Cooperation Framework
ICG	Groupe des crises internationals	International Crisis Group
ICLAC	D'Instituto canadiense de láminas en Construcción de La de Para. d'acero	Instituto canadiense de láminas en acero para la construcción
IDB	Banque Interaméricain de Développement	Inter-American Development Bank
IFS	Institut pour des études fiscales	Institute for Fiscal Studies
IG	Inspecteur Général	Inspector General
IHSI	Institut Haïtien de Statistique et d'Informatique	Haitian Institute of Statistics and Data Processing
ILAC	Consortium Aide Légale Internationale	International Legal Consortium Assistance
IMF	Fonds Monétaire International	International Monetary Fund
IMR	Taux de Mortalite infatilé	Infant mortality rate
LAC		Latin America and the Caribbean
LCR		Latin American and Caribbean Region
LICUS	Pays á faible Revenu etdifficultés	Low Income Countries Under Stress
MAST	Ministère des affaires sociales et d'emploi	Ministry of Social Affairs and Employment
MICIVIH	La Mission Civile Internationale de la L'OEA et la mission internationale des Nations Unies	The OAS/UN International Civilian Mission
MINUSTAH	Mission de stabilisation des Nations Unies en Haïti	United Nations Stabilization Mission in Haiti
NCHR	Coalition nationale pour les droites humains en Haiti	National Coalition for Haitian Rights
NGO	Organisation nonne gouvernementale (ONG)	Nongovernmental organization
NSPs	Non Secteur D'État Dans La Disposition De Service	Non-state service providers
OAS	Organisation des états américains	Organization of American States
OPs	Organisations Populaires	Popular Organizations
PAHO	Organisation Pan-Américaine de la Santé	Pan American Health Organization
PCHI		The Distribution of Per Capita Household Income
PPP	Parité du pouvoir d'achat	Purchasing Power Parity
PREM		Poverty Reduction and Economic Management

PRSP	Papier De Stratégie De Réduction de Pauvreté	Poverty Reduction Strategy Paper
P0		Headcount Poverty Ratio
P1		Poverty Gap Index
P2		Squared Poverty Gap Index
RI	Réfugiés Internationaux	Refugees International
RNDDH	Le Réseau National De la Défense de Droits de l'homme	The National Human Rights Defense Network
RSF	Reporters sans Frontieres	Reporters without Borders
RDNP	Rassemblement des Democrates Nationaux Progressistes	
UN	Les Nations Unies	United Nations
UNDP	Programme des Nations Unies pour le développement	United Nations Development Programme
UNICEF	Le Fonds des Nations Unies pour l'enfance	The United Nations Children's Fund
UNMIH	Mission des Nations Unies en Haïti	United Nations mission to Haiti
UNPOL	Force de police de l'ONU	UN Police force
USD	Dollars des Etats-Unis	United States dollars
USAID	Agence des Etats-Unis pour le développement international	United States Agency for International Development
VAT	Taxe à la valeur ajoutée (TVA)	Value Added Tax
VSN/VNS	Volontaires de la Sécurité Nationale	National Security Volunteers
WBI	Institut de la Banque Mondiale	World Bank Institute
WDI	Indicateurs pour le Développement	World Development Indicators
WFP	Programme mondial d'l'Alimentation	World Food Program

CURRENCY EQUIVALENTS
Currency Unit – Gourde (G)

EXCHANGE RATE
2001 G23.35 = US$1
2002 G28.20 = US$1
2003 G35.95 = US$1
2004 G37 = US$1
2005 G40 = US$1
2006 G41.9 = US$1

WEIGHTS AND MEASURES
Metric System

FISCAL YEAR
January 1–December 31

Executive Summary

By Dorte Verner and Stephanie Kuttner

Haiti is a resilient society whose rural communities in particular have developed coping mechanisms in response to a long history of underdevelopment and political instability. The country's religious, cultural, and artistic life is highly diverse and vibrant. Like other fragile states, however, Haiti is also beset by widespread poverty and inequality, economic decline and unemployment, poor governance, and violence. This Country Social Analysis[1] examines Haiti's conflict-poverty trap from the perspective of the triangle of factors that have been identified as its main components: (a) demographic and socioeconomic factors at the individual and household levels; (b) the state's institutional capacity to provide public goods and manage social risks; and (c) the agendas and strategies of political actors. The report's three main chapters explore the nature of these components, and a closing chapter considers the linkages among them.

The Haitian People: Demographic and Socioeconomic Outcomes and Risks

This section addresses the main demographic and socioeconomic factors that contribute to Haiti's conflict-poverty trap. The population growth rate is highest in the cities, and in the metropolitan area in particular. Port-au-Prince now scores highly on known demographic risk factors for violent conflict, including a very young population profile, high population turnover because of high in- and out-migration, and poverty. New migrants continue to be attracted to the area by higher levels of infrastructure and services, greater access to formal and skilled jobs, and lower poverty levels than all other parts of the country.

Demographic Trends

Haiti's rapidly growing population is increasing competition for scarce resources in a poor country where such resources are limited. At Haiti's current population growth rate of 2.2 percent a year, the number of inhabitants, now about 8 million, could reach about 12.3 million by 2030. The country's rapid rate of population growth, combined with poor economic performance, is lowering per capita GDP, which has fallen by about 50 percent to $332 in the last two decades. Of all sectors, agriculture has been the hardest hit.

In the last two decades there has been a very raid rate of urbanization in Haiti, especially in the metropolitan area. Some 40 percent of Haitians lived in urban areas in 2003, up from 25 percent in 1982. Moreover, Haiti is still far from achieving a demographic transition, since

---

1. The Country Social Analysis (CSA) is a new analytical instrument launched by the World Bank to provide a country-level understanding of the social, economic, and institutional context of development. The CSA analyzes two principal dimensions of development: (i) social diversity, assets, and livelihoods; and (ii) power, governance and institutions. The specific foci and relative emphasis of these components are determined by the country context and Bank portfolio.

children and youth still account for roughly 50 percent of the population. Extremely poor households have about twice as many children as do the nonpoor. Most Haitians lack pensions, social security and savings, and thus children are often the only security for old age.

Poverty and Inequality

In 2001, 49 percent of all Haitian households lived in extreme poverty, with wide differences among localities and regions. On the basis of a US$1 a day extreme poverty line, 20, 56, and 58 percent of households in metropolitan, urban, and rural areas, respectively, were extremely poor. Most of the approximately 3.9 million who are extremely poor live in rural areas. Poverty is especially extensive in the Northeast and Northwest regions. Income inequality partly explains why Haiti's poverty indicators are worse than those in countries that have similar per capita incomes. Income distribution is extremely unequal in Haiti: in 2001, the Gini coefficient for the country as a whole was 0.66, which is among the highest in the world.

Social indicators such as literacy, life expectancy, infant mortality, and child malnutrition also reveal that poverty is widespread. About 4 in every 10 people cannot read and write; some 20 percent of children suffer from malnutrition; nearly half the population has no healthcare; and more than four-fifths do not have access to clean drinking water. The good news is that poverty measured by these non-income poverty indicators has declined in the last three decades. Nonetheless, the gap between the rich and poor, and among regions, remains wide.

Residence in rural areas does not in itself affect the probability of being poor, and those engaged in agriculture are not more likely to experience poverty than those engaged in services and industry. The likelihood of falling below the poverty line in rural areas depends on educational attainment, skills and so on. Female-headed households in rural areas are more likely to be poor than male-headed households. Poverty, moreover, is more prevalent among those with low levels of education. Social capital protects against poverty in rural areas but not to a statistically significant degree in urban areas. In rural, urban and metropolitan areas, migration and education are the factors that most reduce the likelihood of falling into poverty.

Migration and the Endowment and Distribution of Assets and Resources

Livelihoods in Haiti are determined by three key factors: assets, which can be sold to smooth out consumption when the household is adversely affected by a natural disaster or economic slump; access to labor markets, infrastructure, and services that can improve the opportunities for income generation; and migration. Poor households have very little or no access to many of these livelihood-improving factors.

For a large proportion of Haitians, migration is a coping mechanism in the face of poverty and a lack of opportunities. Many move to the capital, which absorbs more than 75,000 migrants every year despite grim living conditions in the slum areas. Most migrants in Haiti are self-selected economic migrants. On average, migrants have more education than those who stay behind. Moreover, migrants have a higher probability of finding jobs than non-migrants, and are more likely to find work in the higher-paid nonfarm sector.

International migration has affected the Haitian economy and the welfare of Haitian households for decades. Haiti is the world's most remittance-dependent country as measured by remittances' share of household income and of GDP. Remittances from the diaspora constitute the most important private risk management and social protection system for Haitian households. Some 30 percent of all households and 44 percent of metropolitan households receive remittances from expatriates. These transfers total about US$800 million annually and account for about 30 percent of household income. Although remittances are an important source of income for many families, emigration also gives rise to lack of qualified workers or a brain drain. For youth, the lack of parental role models (particularly fathers) caused by emigration leaves an even bigger gap.

Access to assets such as education and infrastructural services is highly unequal and strongly correlated with poverty in Haiti. The rural poor in particular lack access to potable water, electricity, and roads. Although overall educational attainment has increased in recent decades, there is substantial variation in attainment and school attendance across regions; children and youth in the poorest regions lag behind their peers in richer regions. Moreover, the children of poor households have less education than their nonpoor peers. Access to safe water and electricity is another significant challenge. Only 7.9 percent of the rural population has access to safe water, compared to 28 percent of those in the metropolitan area. Electricity supply is the public service most marked by unequal access between rural and metropolitan areas: most (91 percent) of the urban population have access to electricity, but the figure falls to 10 percent among the rural population. Moreover, only about 8 percent of Haitians have access to a paved road, and just 3 percent have a telephone. Finally, the extremely poor have much more restricted access to services than do the nonpoor.

Labor is poor people's most abundant asset and it accounts for most of their total income. Nonetheless, the poor are constrained in their labor use in several ways: lack of jobs, low wages, and wage discrimination, especially for women. Many Haitian workers are poor despite working full time, and thus it is important that the quality of jobs, as well as their quantity, is raised. The challenge of job-creation, therefore, is to increase worker productivity and increase opportunities in the labor market for competitive wages, so as to lift workers and their households out of poverty.

Employment analyses suggest that the three key determinants of access to higher-paid employment in Haiti are education, gender, and migration status. Unemployment and underemployment are serious problems, particularly in urban areas. The unemployment rate is highest in urban areas: 49 and 37 percent in metropolitan and other urban areas, respectively, compared to 36 percent in rural areas.

In total, each year more than 100,000 job-seekers enter a metropolitan labor market where there are very few opportunities and a high rate of unemployment. The capital's labor market has fewer total wage jobs than the number of new entrants every two years, and fewer skilled jobs than *one* year of new entrants. Migration and remittances have spurred expansion in areas such as home-building and banking, which has created jobs for construction and business workers. However, most new entrants to the labor market join the estimated one million Haitians in the informal sector who are engaged in a multitude of occupations, from self-employed traders and artisans to casual laborers. Very few formal sector jobs are available.

Haitian youth face a number of challenges, such as unemployment and HIV/AIDs. Youth who leave school are likely to end up being inactive or unemployed. The youth unemployment rate is 47 percent, the highest in Latin America and the Caribbean (LAC) and nearly three times that of the older cohort (the 35–44 age group). The unemployment rate is highest among women across the country and among youth in Port-au-Prince. In many households, youth face the challenges arising from the absence of the father or both parents, drug abuse, early childbearing, and domestic violence. Haiti also has the highest prevalence of HIV/AIDS in the LAC region, and health services are weak or inaccessible for much of the population.

Social Cohesion and Violence

Rural Haiti remains relatively peaceful and has a tradition of strong social cohesion. Especially in fragile states, the ability of communities and households to work and live together is essential to maintaining people's livelihoods, security, and welfare. Social capital indicators that measure levels of trust and reciprocity suggest that robust cohesion on the community level has been crucial in preventing Haiti's institutional-political crisis from deteriorating into broad social collapse or civil war. There are, however, sharp urban-rural differences: people in rural areas feel far safer in their daily lives than do urban residents.

In conjunction with state fragility, political tensions and widespread poverty, rapid urbanization can compound an explosive social situation. Data show that metropolitan residents live in fear of crime and violence, despite higher material living conditions than in rural areas. Respondents in urban slum areas have pointed to multiple causes of violence but concur on the importance of unemployment as a fundamental driver.

A direct indicator of trust and social cohesion is whether people feel safe or afraid in various social situations. As many as 58 percent of residents in the metropolitan area feel unsafe "often or most of the time" in their own home, compared to 15 percent in rural areas. While a significant minority in rural areas also expresses fear of visiting markets and other towns, the data show that fear is not a major and daily concern for three-quarters of the rural population.

Violence is undermining development in Haiti. Domestic violence against women and children is the most prevalent form of violence: 35 percent of women over the age of 15 have been victims of physical violence. As regards homicide rates, Haiti is estimated to have 34 homicides per 100,000 citizens, which is somewhat higher than the regional average of 22.9 per 100,000.

Unconsolidated democratic institutions and "entrepreneurs of violence" have undermined political leadership. Within a year of the country's 1990 elections, democracy was brutally repressed by the army and its supporters, using armed paramilitary groups that have been a feature of Haitian politics since Duvalier's *tonton macoutes*. After President Aristide's return in 1994, democratic consolidation was undermined by deep conflicts among erstwhile democratic allies. The result was a political stalemate that lasted until his departure in 2004 and that stalled progress in poverty reduction, economic growth and state building. Moreover, the stalemate transformed important parts of the democratic movement—elements within the urban popular organizations—into violent government enforcers and criminal gangs that struggled for control of territory and state favors, particularly in urban slums and "popular areas."

The pool of potential recruits for crime and violence thus continues to grow, while the opportunity costs of participating in illegal activities or political violence are low. As the population shifts from rural to urban areas, the robust social cohesion that has characterized rural areas becomes less effective in mitigating social dislocation. This places a heavy burden on state institutions to provide basic services that alleviate demographic and socioeconomic pressures, and to mitigate the negative outcomes of crime and conflict. But the state's institutional capacity to provide basic services, and to establish security and the rule of law, will require significant strengthening if Haiti is to break out of its conflict-poverty trap.

Governance and Institutions

Institutions *matter* for social and economic development, and are crucial for state building. Institutions have the potential to mitigate the risk factors of violence and conflict that emanate from the socioeconomic and demographic context. The Haitian state, however, has only a limited capacity to establish law and order, or to create conditions for economic growth and poverty reduction. Progress in breaking out of the conflict-poverty trap demands attention to the restoration of core state functions in these areas.

To understand the Haitian state's capacity to be a driver of development, its financial constraints must first be noted. Haiti's GDP is extremely low and has been in decline since 1980. In 2005, central government revenues were only 9 percent of GDP, compared to an average of 18 percent among other low-income countries. Only 1.8 percent of revenues derive from taxes on income, profits, or capital. Central government expenditures have fluctuated sharply—between 9 and 16 percent of GDP in recent years—largely as a result of volatility in external assistance. That volatility stems from difficult partnerships with donors who have periodically withdrawn or redirected development assistance in response to political crises and insecurity. Thus a weak domestic revenue base, unstable external flows, and poor expenditure targeting have left spending on education, health, and infrastructure in Haiti below the average of low-income countries.

The state's territorial outreach is limited. The 1987 constitution provides for an elaborate regional and local governance structure. This has never been implemented, however, except at the lowest levels (section communal, commune), where many local councils have been active despite a lack of financial and material resources.

Infrastructure and Basic Services

In response to the extremely limited public sector provision of infrastructures and basic services throughout the country, the non-state sector has expanded rapidly to attend to unmet needs, especially for health and education services. This may account for the observed improvement in some social indicators. Yet critical gaps in coverage persist in terms of access for the poorest and the overall quality of services for the majority.

The role of the Haitian state in primary education is uniquely low from a global perspective. Of the world's 20 poorest countries, Haiti is the only one in which more than 50 percent of children are enrolled in non-state schools. A snapshot of the education sector reveals an elite category of private schools (usually religious and urban-based) that have established themselves at the top of the pile, but are affordable to only a small segment of the population. These are followed by a large group of public schools that occupy the middle of the range, and then by the vast majority of private schools at the bottom. Public schools exist mainly in urban areas and 92 percent of all schools are non-state, the vast majority of which do not receive public subsidies. Among all primary and secondary school students, 82 percent attend private, fee-paying schools.

State health service provision is similarly limited. Only about 30 percent of health facilities in Haiti are public, and most of them are in urban areas. Nongovernmental organizations (NGOs) provide an estimated 70 percent of health services in rural areas and focus in particular on primary health care, including reproductive health, drug counseling, infant care, and HIV/AIDS screening. There are a number of hospitals run by private foundations but the state retains the main responsibility for secondary and tertiary care, as well as for overall oversight and referral.

Recent surveys examining the role of non-state service providers in rural areas and poor neighborhoods in Port-au-Prince have found a strong presence of community organizations in areas such as sanitation, drinking water, healthcare, education, and even electricity provision. Public utilities are the main providers of water and electricity but that circumstance does not ensure equal access. The diverse and unregulated nature of basic service-provision can be exploited by political interests that use access as a means of bestowing patronage, garnering support, and gaining leverage. Access to services is patchy, unstable, and unequal, reflecting political considerations in initial provision, poor maintenance capacity, a low level of coordination, and the violence and crime that affect service supply and demand. Given the state's limited resources and capacity to provide services directly, development efforts should focus on improving the policy guidelines, coordination mechanisms, and regulatory frameworks for public-private partnerships.

Security and the Rule of Law

Security and the rule of law are not only crucial to ensuring justice and safety; they are also essential in creating an enabling environment for investments, economic growth, and development. However, private systems of violence linked to political and criminal activities have become decentralized and widespread; Haiti now has more private security personnel than police officers. The institutions responsible for establishing security and the rule of law—the police, judiciary and prisons—have largely collapsed, and to some degree they have become a source of insecurity themselves. Political interference and corruption have undermined previous reform efforts and brought about the rapid withdrawal of international assistance, with further destabilizing effects.

Haiti has one of the world's weakest police forces. There are 63 police officers per 100,000 people, less than a quarter of the regional average of 283 per 100,000 and only a third of the average for sub-Saharan African countries. Moreover, a significant number of members of the Haitian National Police (HNP) are alleged to be involved in criminal and violent activities, including direct involvement in the past year's wave of kidnappings, according to human rights organizations and police officials themselves. The United Nations Stabilization Mission in Haiti (MINUSTAH) is mandated to support national authorities in the reform of the HNP, but it has not had executive authority over the national police force for the purposes of overseeing and monitoring the latter's activities. There are increasing calls within Haiti and among the international community for MINUSTAH's mandate to be strengthened in this regard.

Haiti's judiciary is similarly weakened by corruption and frequent political interference, which have undermined the institution's independence and constrained the success of previous reform efforts. The justice system suffers from the obsolescence of many laws, the absence of basic guarantees, poorly trained and paid judicial officers, and the advanced state of deterioration of its physical infrastructure. As a result, access to law and justice is difficult and random. Moreover, there is only limited integration of the police, judiciary, and prisons into a functioning criminal justice system or *chaîne pénale*. Communication breakdowns between the investigative "judicial police," the prosecutor's office, court clerks and the prison administration result in long delays in the administration of justice and a pretrial detention rate of almost 80 percent.

The state's ability to provide basic public goods has thus been undermined by a history of neglect, political capture and corruption, and compounded by difficult donor partnerships As regards the state's administrative capacity, the territorial reach of state institutions is minimal outside major urban centers, decentralization has not been implemented, and the state has been unable to provide basic services or infrastructures to large portions of the population. A diverse and vibrant non-state sector has filled some of the gaps in health and education, but these efforts have been largely uncoordinated and unregulated. The result has been a substantial variation in the quality of the services provided and significant gaps in services for certain regions and vulnerable groups. The institutions responsible for providing the essential public goods of security and the rule of law (namely, the police and judiciary) are largely ineffective and suffer repeated problems of political interference and corruption. Above all, core state institutions remain weak, and the impacts of past technical assistance programs have been largely lost. Before beginning large-scale capacity building programs, government and donors must establish firm oversight and mutual accountability mechanisms to obviate the recurrence of practices that weaken institutions and perpetuate the conflict-poverty trap.

Political Actors and Strategies

Twenty years have passed since the 1986 ouster of Jean-Claude "Baby Doc" Duvalier created a window of opportunity to establish a more stable and democratic form of governance. Yet, Haiti's highly-polarized politics has complicated efforts to address the country's complex and deeply rooted development challenges.

The 1987 constitution provides for a clear separation of executive, judicial and legislative powers, as well as decentralized governance structures. In practice, however, politics in Haiti lacks a predictable system of rules. Political stability will remain illusive without the establishment of an equilibrium among the competing forces within society—including class forces that historically have pitted a small political and economic elite against the vastly larger urban and rural poor. Haitian politics swings between two key dangers: capture by privileged elites who harness government to protect their dominant position in society; and populism that neglects the country's long-term institutional and economic development while paying lip service to the poor. The 2006 elections do not themselves ensure national reconciliation, but Haiti's return to elected rule does create opportunities for the consolidation of democratic institutions and processes.

Strong national leadership is crucial to achieving a turnaround in Haiti. Entrepreneurs of violence have taken advantage of political instability and weak state institutions to manipulate popular grievances for political and criminal ends. Breaking free of Haiti's poverty-conflict trap will require capable national political leadership that is committed to the consolidation of democratic institutions and processes. In a context of very difficult socioeconomic conditions, high social risks, defunct state institutions, extremely limited budget resources, and political polarization, Haiti's leaders face enormous challenges. The

2006 electoral process, however, has created new opportunities for reform, reconciliation and partnerships.

Conclusion: Breaking the Conflict-Poverty Trap

Haiti's social resilience and social capital, its vibrant cultural life and improvements in social indicators are keystones to draw upon in breaking the conflict-poverty trap. Haiti's deep and widespread poverty results from a long history of failure to establish even basic enabling conditions for broad-based social and economic development. The state has struggled to provide basic services to the population and has been dominated by a small elite that has made limited investments in infrastructure and basic services. Development, poverty reduction and conflict prevention will not be possible without a focus on strengthening the state's capacity to provide basic public goods, including security and the rule of law. Its financial and managerial resources must be used with an exceptionally strong sense of priority. In the past, however, efforts to restore state functions have been undermined by political interference and corruption, which in turn prompted the withdrawal and redirection of donor support.

A reduction in violence and an improvement in security conditions are of paramount importance in fostering sustainable development in Haiti. Very poor urban neighborhoods are explosive points of conflict in the country's development crisis, combining demographic, socioeconomic, institutional, and political risk factors. Violence and insecurity in the Port-au-Prince slums in particular have undermined the political process, fuelled conflict, and negatively affected development and reconstruction efforts. Joint multisectoral interventions in key urban areas (including Cité Soleil) that combine security and poverty reduction objectives will be essential for creating the conditions necessary for broad-based national development strategies.

The most important factor for breaking out of Haiti's poverty-conflict trap cannot be provided by donors but only by Haitians themselves: good leadership. Donors can support good leadership by establishing incentives that reward good governance and penalize the opposite. Because of the centrality of corruption in undermining good leadership, transparency in public finances should be a foundation for the Bank and other donors' assistance to a new Haitian government.

Haiti's development crisis is so multifaceted, and the country's needs are so many, that prioritizing reconstruction efforts and development assistance has proven difficult. This report argues that the focus should be on the restoration of core state functions—the provision of the public goods of security and the rule of law, infrastructure and basic services. Among the triangle of risk factors in the poverty-conflict trap, institutional capacity building is a key entry point for breaking the cycle; improving demographic and socioeconomic outcomes and supporting political dialogue remain longer-term objectives. Institutional reform itself, however, requires a long-term engagement. National planning and international assistance should build on the existing International Cooperation Framework by prioritizing resources and monitoring progress, such that both donors and government can be held accountable for results.

CHAPTER 1

Introduction

By Dorte Verner and Willy Egset

Haiti holds a unique place in modern world history as the first independent black republic, established in 1804 following the only successful slave revolution against colonial rule. Undoubtedly, this historic accomplishment has helped build national pride and solidarity across economic and social distinctions in Haiti, and is reflected in the country's vibrant cultural life. But as a stark reminder of the republic's troubled history, the bicentennial of independence was overshadowed by violence and political instability that resulted in the fall of President's Aristide's government in February 2004. The sources of both Haiti's strong social resilience and the recurrent political instability can be located in the country's difficult independence process, which is discussed briefly below as a backdrop to this report's more contemporary focus. Today, the report argues, poverty, institutional weakness, and urban violence continue to sustain Haiti's *conflict-poverty trap* in ever shifting ways. Yet Haitians continue to cope by means of informal social mechanisms and migration abroad. This report analyzes these challenges and opportunities in Haiti's development trajectory and proposes strategic development priorities to reinforce strengths and mitigate weaknesses. The analytical approach is described in more detail below, following a brief historical introduction.[2]

Historical Background: Origins of the Rural-Urban Divide

The Republic of Haiti emerged from a colonial order that established economic and social conditions for its post-independence development. Haiti is more known for its early colonial-era dominance in sugar production, but the rapid growth of coffee production

---

2. The historical background section is based largely on Trouillot (1990) and Lundahl (1979).

in the second part of the eighteenth century transformed Haitian society in several ways (Trouillot 1990). The expansion of coffee production to meet soaring international demand attracted a new class of French migrants with more humble backgrounds than the traditional French sugar aristocracy. Together with freed people of mixed ancestry, they established small coffee estates in the country's mountainous interior, thereby providing a basis for peasant production outside the sugar plantations of the coastal plains. This development reinforced another practice, whereby slaves were given garden plots for small-scale farming on land that was unfit for larger-scale production and that was more amply available in the interior. Coffee production made the interior a significant economic locus and helped turn an increasing number of producers against French colonial rule. France's trade monopoly cut off producers from valuable markets in other European countries and the United States. Haitian nationalism was also growing, forging a sense of identity that—with the independence process—came to be seen as essentially black, even among the lighter skinned economic elite.[3]

Despite this growing nationalism, Haiti's political and economic leaders and most of the population were set on different courses. The revolutionary wars destroyed much of Haiti's physical and human capital. Plantations were ruined; a third of the slave population was killed, and many escaped to the mountains or enrolled in revolutionary armies; almost the entire white administrative class disappeared; and foreign trade practically came to a standstill. Slavery was abolished but the wars had a disastrous impact on the country's economy from a fiscal perspective. Hence Haiti's new leaders, from L'Ouverture during the wars and continuing under Dessalines from 1804, were determined to re-establish large-scale export-oriented plantations to restore the country's economic strength. Former plantation land owned by whites was confiscated by the state, which led efforts to restore the plantations. However, the availability of land in the interior, and the former slaves' aversion to plantation work, made it impossible to secure the necessary voluntary labor. Hence the introduction of the *fermage* system, whereby every person who was not in the army or in urban trade was attached to a plantation under strict supervision and control. This re-establishment of export production through coercion met with some initial success, but for a number of economic and political reasons[4] the restoration policy proved futile and land was gradually redistributed into peasant plots. By the end of the nineteenth century, Haitian agriculture was characterized almost entirely by smallholding peasant production geared to subsistence and local markets.[5] The country's financial situation remained weak throughout the century as a result of the loss of export revenues, an international diplomatic boycott,[6] a heavy indemnity levied by France against its losses in Haiti, and declining terms of trade.

These circumstances solidified a widening breach between the rural, peasant majority and the increasingly urban, political and economic elite (Lundahl 1979). The peasantry, having acquired land and freedom, had no incentive to engage with the authorities and

---

3. The *grand blancs, petits blancs,* and the *affranchis/gen de coleur.*
4. Land was amply available, terms of trade unfavorable.
5. New attempts were made to restore plantation production during the U.S. occupation (1915–34), resulting in a broad peasant uprising (Lundahl 1979).
6. France and the United States with held recognition until 1825 and 1862, respectively.

withdrew to a relative seclusion that was interrupted by sporadic rebellions when either their land or liberty were perceived to be threatened. The rural economy, which accounted for more than 90 percent of the population, entered a low or zero-growth equilibrium and attracted little private investment. The elite lost material interest in an agricultural sector that produced no significant farm-level profit, and instead taxed the sector as a whole via the state administration. Former landowners and other members of the economic elite thus turned away from a productive engagement in agriculture and focused on political and administrative positions. As political conflict and corruption intensified during the first century after independence, there was a further decline in incentives to develop rather than tax the rural sector. Since those living in the countryside were politically excluded and economically exploited through the public tax system, they avoided the political violence that was mostly concentrated in the capital, Port-au-Prince, and other major towns.[7]

The nature of this political-economic system was always shifting but some basic aspects of the spoils system remained unchanged throughout the U.S. occupation (1915–34) and subsequent administrations. The system was taken to extremes by the Duvalier regime (1957–86). As discussed later in this report, the regime was not only more brutal than earlier governments; its repressive capacity was also used to secure personal gain on an unprecedented scale, thereby contributing to the legacy of corruption that besets Haiti to this day.

This report will show that many legacies of Haiti's past have continued to pose challenges to its post-authoritarian development, both politically and economically. Poverty is greater in rural areas, reflecting a history of government neglect that is evident in a lack of basic public goods (notably physical infrastructure), law enforcement, judicial institutions, environmental protection, and regulatory frameworks. Basic healthcare, education, and other services are supplied by a patchy system of public and private (for profit) providers and nongovernmental organizations (NGOs), largely without government oversight. As a result, large parts of the population lack access to quality primary education and health services (see Chapter 3). Today, two-thirds of Haitians still live in rural areas and most of them make their living directly or indirectly through small-scale farming. As a result of population pressures, environmental degradation and land erosion, increased education, and a lack of opportunities to escape rural poverty, agriculture is becoming a less attractive choice.

Inequality is almost equally high *within* the rural and urban sectors, but most glaring are the enormous differences between rural and metropolitan areas in income and poverty levels; social indicators (literacy, malnutrition, infant mortality); and access to services (education, healthcare) and infrastructure (water, electricity, roads, telephones)—see Chapter 2. Living conditions in the capital area's many large slums are harsh, but these urban-rural differences and the concentration of jobs and opportunities in the metropolitan area attract vast numbers of migrants every year. Poverty, inequality, and the absence of social and economic opportunities spawn frustrations that can be exploited by those willing to undermine the formal political process in order to gain power. Haiti's state institutions have only a limited capacity to manage conflicts, address grievances, and deter the

---

7. The exception was peasant participation in the so-called *cacos* rebellions in the late nineteenth and early twentieth centuries.

violent potential that arises from these socioeconomic conditions. The state's capacity is further constrained by a very weak domestic revenue base and the volatility of aid flows. The transition from dictatorship in 1986 offered an opportunity for change, but progress has been thwarted by recurring conflict, political instability, and resource constraints. In 2004, Haiti again underwent a violent regime change, followed by a period of increased violence and insecurity, particularly in Port-au-Prince.

Analytical Framework

Fragile states such as Haiti are characterized by widespread poverty and inequality, economic decline and unemployment, institutional weakness and poor governance, violence, lawlessness, and persistent conflict. This report will explore how the links between these factors affect Haiti's development challenge, and provide the empirical underpinnings and strategic priorities for poverty reduction and conflict prevention. Violent internal conflicts are statistically concentrated in poor countries, but poverty alone does not *cause* conflict. A large body of recent research concurs that the relationships among economic, institutional, and political factors in conflict are complex, interdependent, and context-specific (Elbadawi 1992; Collier 1999; Collier and Hoeffler 2000; Easterly and Gatti 2000; Berdal and Malone 2001; and Collier and others 2003). In most cases, violent conflict is a symptom of multifaceted development and governance malfunctions. In such fragile environments, the design and timing of international development assistance can play a critical role in addressing the root causes of conflict. Yet, economic assistance may also be ineffective and counterproductive if it is not adapted to a country's specific circumstances (Vallings and Moreno-Torres 2005).

This report therefore examines Haiti's situation from the perspective of a triangle of factors that have been identified as critical determinants of the development trajectory of fragile states,[8] including: (a) demographic and socioeconomic factors at the individual and household levels; (b) the capacity of core state institutions to provide basic services, including security and the rule of law; and (c) the agendas and strategies of political actors. It also examines the interaction of these three factors, as illustrated in Figure 1.1.

The report discusses these factors in its three main chapters and the conclusion. Following an overview in the introduction, Chapter 2 addresses socioeconomic and demographic factors in an effort to further understanding of trends in population, poverty, and employment by identifying the characteristics of the poor and analyzing the determinants of poverty (Buvinic and Morrison n.d.; Collier and others 2003; Kelly 2000; Collier 2000). These socioeconomic and demographic outcomes are further analyzed with a view to explaining how, as direct and indirect risk factors, they contribute to crime and conflict. On the demographic front, population growth and density, as well as migration, are important conflict risk factors if they are not matched by equal or preferably higher rates of economic

---

8. See, for example, Collier and others (2003). The authors of this landmark study identify key causes of violent conflict as a "lethal cocktail" of "low and declining incomes, badly distributed, [that] create a pool of impoverished and disaffected young men who can be cheaply recruited by 'entrepreneurs of violence.' In such conditions the state is also likely to be weak, non-democratic, and incompetent, offering little impediment to the escalation of rebel violence, and maybe even provoking it" (Collier et al. 2003).

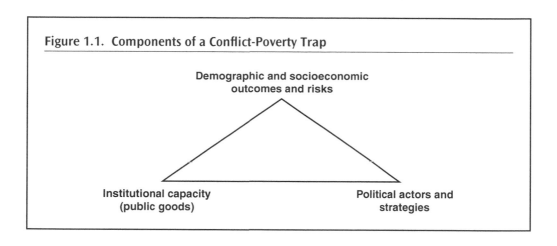

Figure 1.1. Components of a Conflict-Poverty Trap

Demographic and socioeconomic
outcomes and risks

Institutional capacity
(public goods)

Political actors and
strategies

growth. Among economic factors, inequality appears to be a crucial element that increases *crime* (both violent and otherwise), but that has only indirect effects on violent *political conflict*. The opposite is true for poverty: poverty reduction (that is, higher per capita income) significantly reduces violent conflict risk but does not have a measurable effect on reducing criminal violence (Collier and Hoeffler 2002). These economic variables themselves are negatively affected by conflict, contributing to the self-perpetuating nature of conflict-poverty traps.[9]

Chapter 3 addresses public governance functions that are considered essential for reconstruction and development in fragile states, mainly the core state functions of providing the basic public goods needed to foster economic growth and ensure human security, including the deterrence of violent crime and destabilizing conflict. The need for stable and effective state institutions is particularly string in countries facing significant challenges of social and economic inclusion and a high risk of conflict. This chapter examines the state's administrative and territorial reach and its ability to provide basic public services, including security and the rule of law.

Chapter 4 assesses the role of political factors in Haiti's development crisis. Again, understanding these factors is essential to an appreciation of socioeconomic processes and reform prospects in general, and of conflict dynamics in particular. Public governance institutions are ultimately designed by political actors representing social constituencies. An existing institutional architecture reflects past political power structures; the evolving nature of the power structure will determine future institutional change. Similarly, economic deprivation is neither a sufficient nor a necessary condition for collective political action. Rather, political action—whether for reform or revolt—is the result of political organization. Thus Chapter 4 examines political actors, their social constituencies, and their agendas, including those actors involved in recent violence. Chapter 5 concludes by drawing together the three components of Haiti's poverty-conflict trap and suggests entry points for breaking this cycle.

---

9. Ominously for Haiti, Collier (1999) finds that long conflicts tend to produce a post-conflict recovery effect, whereas short and recurrent conflicts—which are typical of Haiti—lead to continued economic decline.

CHAPTER 2

The Haitian People: Demographics, Poverty, and Socioeconomic Outcomes and Risks

By Dorte Verner

This chapter analyzes demographic, poverty and socioeconomic outcomes as the first dimension of Haiti's conflict-poverty trap.[10] It first considers demographic trends and the risks evident in high population growth and density, rapid urbanization (particularly to the metropolitan area), and high fertility rates (particularly among the poor). The second section presents data on poverty and inequality in Haiti, comparing the characteristics of poor urban and rural households, and also considers regional differences. The third section analyzes the distribution of assets in terms of human capital (health and education), as well as access to basic infrastructure services (water, electricity, roads) and employment opportunities. It also considers Haiti's high levels of youth unemployment, which increase the risk of crime and conflict. The fourth section addresses traditional forms of community-level social cohesion and the growing threat posed by urban violence. Together, these factors portray the structural dimensions of poverty and inequality that increase conflict risk in Haiti.

Demographic Trends

Demographic factors have direct and indirect effects on prices, poverty, and conflict risks in Haiti. As the size and age composition of the population changes, so too do the relative size of the labor force and the number of dependents. This affects the dependency ratio of families and therefore their level of poverty. High population growth can also increase

---

10. This chapter is mainly based on Verner (2005).

conflict risk by reducing per capita economic opportunities and creating a large pool of potential recruits (typically, young men below 25 years of age) for criminal and political violence. Some studies, moreover, find that population growth, density, and turnover contribute to increased crime rates and conflict risks by limiting economic opportunities and increasing the supply of potential victims who do not know the perpetrator (Kelly 2000; Collier 2000). Family instability and break-up have been identified as additional demographic risk factors for violence and crime because of the emotional disturbance suffered by children,[11] the subsequent lack of role models, and other effects such as worsened socioeconomic outcomes (Kelly 2000).

Demographic changes affect quantities: number of children, size of the labor force, and number of elderly people. These changes in quantities will generally influence prices in the economy. In particular, changes in the population's growth rate and age structure may have significant effects on the labor supply, savings, household production decisions, and migration. Consequently, demographic changes may have a substantial impact on wage levels and interest rates. Since these prices are important determinants of family income, they are bound to have a profound influence on the level of poverty. Hence demographic changes indirectly impact poverty through their effects on savings, wages, production decisions, and interest rates.

Changing demographics can also have significant effects on the demand for public sector investments and public services, incentives for private sector investments, social and political conflict (see Chapter 4), and labor markets (see below). Thus it is important to look at recent changes in demographic patterns in Haiti's rural and urban areas. The following overview briefly describes the demographic changes that have taken place in the last two decades.[12]

Population, Population Growth and Density, Age Structure, and Urbanization

Haiti is slightly smaller than Wales and its population is growing rapidly (2.2 percent a year). In 1950, the population was estimated at just over 3 million. By 2001, the number had grown to nearly 8 million. With a surface area of just 27,797 square kilometers (km²), Haiti is second only to Barbados as the most densely populated country (306 people per km²) in the Americas.

After expanding at an annual rate of about 1.5 percent between 1950 and 1982, Haiti's population increased by 2.2 percent annually in the period 1982–2003 and reached 7.9 million in 2003 (see Table B.1 in Appendix B). The current population growth rate of more than 2 percent a year suggests that the country's inhabitants could total some 12.3 million by 2030.[13] The indications, however, are that the population growth rate is slowing. Overall, the proportion of the population aged below 15 years is gradually declining. This reflects the twin effects of urbanization (fertility rates are lower in urban areas than in the countryside) and gradually declining fertility rates overall (partly the result of increased educational

---

11. Including exposure to violence at a young age, which is a prime risk factor for violent behavior later in life (Buvinic and Morrison n.d.).

12. This section is based on Verner (2005), which provides more information about demographic trends in Haiti.

13. World Bank: http://genderstats.worldbank.org/hnpstats/HNPDemographic/total.pdf.

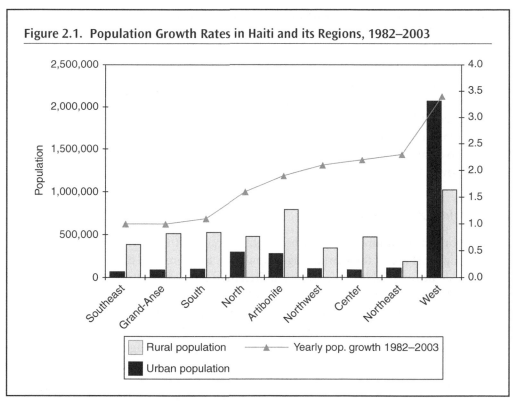

Figure 2.1. Population Growth Rates in Haiti and its Regions, 1982–2003

Source: IHSI 2003.

attainment). The median age increased slightly from 18.5 to 18.9 years between 1994–95 and 2000, revealing the incremental pace of this demographic change (DHS 2000).

During the 1982–2003 period, the poorest region (the Northeast) and the richest region (the West, where Port-au-Prince is located) experienced a higher population growth rate than the country's average of 2.2 percent. In the Southeast and Grand-Anse regions, by contrast, the population grew annually by 1.2 percent below the national average (see Table B.1 in Appendix B and Figure 2.1).

The West and Artibonite regions have the largest shares of population among Haiti's nine regions: 39.0 and 13.5 percent, respectively. In the West region, people mainly reside in Port-au-Prince (Figure 2.1). Finally, demographic analysis reveals a family structure in which most children and youth grow up with only one, or neither, of their parents. In total, 51 percent of all children below 15 years of age, and 61 percent of children in the metropolitan area, do not live with both of their parents. Among these, most live only with their mothers (35 percent of all children in the metropolitan area); a smaller number live with their fathers (8 percent of all children in the metropolitan area); and as many as 17 percent—both in the metropolitan area and nationwide—live with neither parent (DHS 2000).[14]

---

14. Note that only a few of these are "restaveks," domestic child workers, a group of children considered particularly vulnerable and who have been the focus of several advocacy campaigns. Among 5 to 14 year-olds, 3.5 percent are identified as restaveks in the DHS survey (DHS 2000).

Haiti has become far more urbanized in the last two decades because the highest population growth has been in urban areas. In 2003, 40.4 percent of Haitians lived in urban areas, up from 24.5 percent in 1982.[15] Rural Haiti is now home to some 4.7 million people (59.6 percent of the population).[16] The urban population increased from 1.2 million to 3.2 million between 1982 and 2003. In other words, 115,000 people have been added to Haiti's cities every year for the past 21 years. Among the 1.97 million people added to urban areas between 1982 and 2003, 1.3 million (or two-thirds) went to the West region. The metropolitan area has received an average of 75,000 migrants a year in the past 20 years, in addition to a natural growth of nearly 40,000 people a year, bringing its total annual population growth to 115,000 people (see below for more on migration).

Household Size and Fertility

The proportion of children and youth is slightly larger in the countryside than in urban areas. A higher share of the working age population live in urban areas, so urban households should be better able to feed their children than those in rural areas. Hence the overall dependency ratio is larger in rural and non-metropolitan urban areas than in Port-au-Prince. The average household is slightly larger in the former areas (4.6 and 4.7, respectively) than in the capital (4.5).

The typical extremely poor or poor household has more young members than does a nonpoor household. In Haiti, extremely poor households in rural and metropolitan areas have on average 2.2 and 1.7 household members below 15 years of age, respectively.[17] This compares to the average nonpoor household, in which only 0.9 and 1.2 members are below the age of 15 (Tables B.3 and B.4 in Appendix B). Extremely poor households therefore have about twice as many children as do nonpoor households. Most Haitians lack pensions, social security and savings, and thus children are often the only security for old age. An older Haitian woman expressed the matter this way: "It costs a lot to educate a child in Haiti; you have to work very hard. When I helped them with their education, I considered it like putting money into a savings account. My children are my bank account."[18]

The fertility rate has fallen rapidly in recent decades. During the three decades leading to the 1990s the fertility rate fell from 6.3 children per woman in 1960 to 5.4 in 1990, and then to 4.7 in 2000 (World Bank 2004). Women's increased participation in the labor market is an important factor in the decline in the fertility rate.

As educational attainment increases, moreover, the fertility rate drops. The total desired fertility rate is lower than the actual fertility rate, which indicates that there is still a substantial unmet demand for high quality and reliable family planning services, information, and resources.[19] Efforts to close the gap between desired and actual fertility would reduce the high dependency ratio, which is an important driver of poverty. Thus far demographic trends have not lowered the dependency ratio significantly, and therefore they have

---

15. Table B.2 in Appendix B.
16. Figure 2.1 and Table B.1 in Appendix B.
17. See Appendix C for a definition of extremely poor, poor, and nonpoor.
18. Source: http://www.philly.com/mld/inquirer/9102135.htm.
19. Unfortunately, fertility rate microdata are unavailable and thus the analysis cannot be taken further.

contributed negatively to poverty reduction. This trend is likely to intensify in the future if the country does not implement reproductive health programs.

Haitian Poverty and Inequality

Household Income and Income Generation

Except in the metropolitan area, most Haitian households have low annual per capita incomes. In 2001, the median income per capita of extremely poor households (1,080 gourdes) was around one-tenth of the median income of the nonpoor (10,304 gourdes). Median income varies greatly across regions and locations. In 2001, median household income per capita in the metropolitan area (7,293 gourdes) was far higher than elsewhere in Haiti. The households with the lowest median incomes per capita are located in the Northeast region, where they stand at 617 and 804 gourdes in urban and rural areas, respectively (Table 2.1). In the West region, by contrast, the median income per capita of households is 5–6 times higher in rural and urban areas (excluding the metropolitan area) than in the Northeast. These figures reveal how access to imported goods and to a large market like Port-au-Prince can make a difference in people's well-being.

There are significant differences in the distribution of per capita household income (PCHI) by geographic locality. The PCHI of a household in the first decile of the income distribution is 199, 166, and 910 gourdes in rural, urban, and metropolitan areas, respectively (Table 2.2). Hence households on the low end of the income distribution in metropolitan Haiti have much better incomes than those in other urban or rural areas. Rural households are better off than urban households on the low end of the income distribution. The per capita income difference between households in rural and metropolitan areas is fairly constant across the income distribution. At a given location in the distribution of income, metropolitan households earn roughly four times more than households in rural

Table 2.1. Median Annual Income Per Capita, 2001 (gourdes)

Region	Metro.	Urban	Rural	Total Haiti
Artibonite	NA	1,723	2,135	2,000
Center	NA	2,317	2,430	2,390
Grand-Anse	NA	1,654	1,900	1,830
North	NA	3,304	1,585	1,900
Northeast	NA	804	617	672
Northwest	NA	2,471	1,500	1,734
West	7,293	4,015	3,100	4,367
South	NA	2,761	1,696	1,922
Southeast	NA	3,240	2,372	2,508
Haiti	7,293	2,265	2,035	2,403

Source: Authors' calculations based on HLCS 2001.

Table 2.2. Average Income Per Capita by Decile, 2001 (gourdes)

Decile	Metropolitan	Urban	Rural
1	910	166	199
2	1,435	473	524
3	3,074	862	879
4	4,360	1,301	1,306
5	6,177	1,888	1,787
6	8,690	2,638	2,352
7	12,312	3,570	3,100
8	16,915	5,112	4,177
9	25,624	8,469	6,196
10	73,430	28,522	17,177

Source: Authors' calculations based on HLCS 2001.

areas. One important explanatory factor may be the greater number of opportunities in metropolitan Haiti. People living in the metropolitan area have access to more jobs, and the self-employed have access to domestically produced and imported goods that they can resell in the metropolitan market or to other urban and rural markets. This is significantly different from conditions in other areas in Haiti, where very few goods originate (see below for more on income inequality). Self-consumption is part of the reason why the poorest are better off in rural than in urban areas (see Figure 2.2).

Self-employment income, wages, and transfers are crucial to reducing poverty in Haiti. Self-employment is the most important income source for all income levels, although it accounts for more of the total income of the poorest 10 percent of the population (46.7 percent of their total income) than of the richest 10 percent (30.9 percent of their income). Self-consumption is of little importance for the lowest and highest deciles, but accounts for 18–24 percent of total income for deciles 3–7. Private transfers, mostly remittances, are generally the second most important income source, accounting for 26 and 30 percent of the total income of the poorest 10 percent and the richest 10 percent, respectively. Salaries are relatively unimportant for deciles 1–3: less than 6 percent of this group's total income is from wage labor. For the upper deciles, however, salaries are a significant part of total income: 19.3 and 30.7 percent for the top two deciles, respectively.

Farm labor is still the most important income source for Haiti's rural population. Both the poor and nonpoor in rural areas receive the largest share of their total income from activities such as farming and agricultural labor (Table 2.3). Rural dwellers also work as laborers in the nonfarm sector. The extremely poor and nonpoor rural populations receive 26-34 percent of their total income off-farm. Remittances account for 14 percent of the extremely poor's total income. This is 6 percentage points fewer than the share of remittances (20 percent) in the total income of the richest 20 percent of the rural population.

Wages and incomes are crucial to escaping poverty. Comparisons of household heads aged 12 and older at different places in the income distribution show that incomes are by

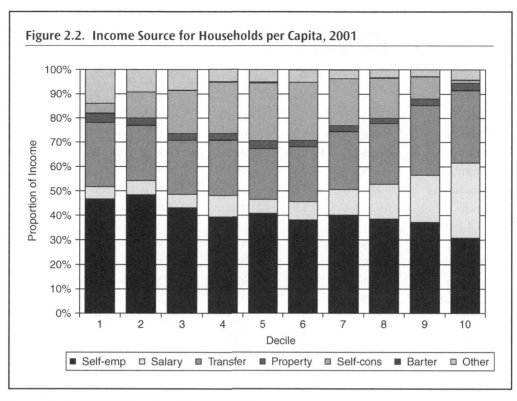

Figure 2.2. Income Source for Households per Capita, 2001

Source: Authors' calculations based on HLCS 2001.

no means determined in the same way for high- and low-paid workers. Residence in rural areas affects income positively for heads in the lowest quintile, everything else equal.

Human capital has proven to be important in enhancing long-term economic growth (Barro 1991; Mankiw, Romer, and Weil 1992). A more educated workforce is likely to be

Table 2.3. Income Source for Households Per Capita 2001 (percent)

Quintile	Rural Population				Whole Population			
	Farm	Off-farm	Remittances	Other	Farm	Off-farm	Remittances	Other
1 (poorest)	39.0	33.6	14.4	13.1	37.2	34.2	15.4	13.2
2	49.2	26.6	14.4	9.9	41.2	30.5	17.7	10.5
3	51.6	25.8	14.7	7.9	43.2	31.1	17.6	8.1
4	51.4	27.0	15.5	6.1	36.6	37.1	18.7	7.7
5 (richest)	37.3	34.4	20.4	7.5	10.9	52.1	27.8	9.3

Note: "Farm" includes own consumption of crops and meat, as well as barter. "Other" refers to transfers other than remittances and property income. "Off-farm" includes all forms of labor income and sales of products.
Source: Authors' calculations based on HLCS 2001.

Table 2.4. Determinants of Income in Haiti, 2001 Quantiles, Dependent Variable: Log Total Income (per capita)[20]

	10th	25th	50th	75th	90th	OLS
Female	5.5	12.9	10.3	0.3	4.0	5.5
Primary	95.2	75.4	82.7	80.6	69.2	88.1
Secondary	331.8	199.9	203.0	220.1	177.5	201.6
Tertiary	1850.5	1319.1	1271.9	1158.9	910.2	1014.3
Industry	47.9	14.8	−16.1	−10.9	−20.8	−17.7
Agriculture	−14.6	−19.9	−34.7	−44.3	−55.5	−50.3
Service	−7.1	−3.9	−14.8	−6.8	−0.9	−9.8
Social capital	19.1	14.7	0.7	−6.2	−7.1	−0.7
Rural	290.9	41.7	19.7	−18.3	−30.1	3.35
R*female	−6.9	−21.5	−21.5	−5.7	−5.2	−14.0
R*primary	−20.1	−19.4	−22.2	−21.3	−13.3	−24.7
R*secondary	−39.5	−17.1	−32.8	−33.3	−14.6	−27.7
R*tertiary	−59.6	−59.2	−72.4	−70.6	−14.0	−61.9
R*industry	−60.3	−37.0	−21.8	−15.2	0.3	−17.5
R*agriculture	−34.9	−14.7	−11.9	17.0	46.1	20.1
R*service	−43.8	−23.7	−25.3	−20.7	−16.5	−25.9
R*social	12.8	11.7	20.5	24.2	14.1	20.8

Note: Excluded categories: no completed education and public. Number of observations: 7,099.
Source: Extract from Table 9.12 in Verner (2005) based on HLCS 2001. Initial estimates similar to Mincer equation—including household size, etc.

more productive, flexible, and innovative, and to facilitate the adoption and use of new technologies. Because of the increasing speed of technological change faced by firms and farms today, as well as international economic integration, workers need more skills if those firms and farms are to be competitive. One reason for this is that employees with more skills can adjust more easily than less skilled workers to changes in their firm's or farm's economic and technological environment.[21] More educated individuals earn higher incomes than their less educated peers. In 2001, returns to primary, secondary, and tertiary education were positive for all in the analyzed quantiles (see Table 2.4), indicating that

---

20. The wage determination process is analyzed using the quantile regression methodology (Appendix C).
21. One issue that needs to be mentioned concerns the endogeneity of education in the regressions. There is vast evidence of a positive correlation between earnings and education. Social scientists, however, are cautious in drawing a strong inference about the causal effect of education. In the absence of experimental evidence, it is difficult to determine whether the higher earnings observed for better educated employees are caused by their higher level of completed education, or whether employees with greater earnings capacity have chosen to acquire more education. Card (1998) surveys the literature on the causal relationship between education and earnings, and finds that the average marginal return to education is not much below the estimate that emerges from standard human capital earnings function studies.

completion of at least a few years of education contributes more to incomes than no education at all. Furthermore, overall the premium is rapidly increasing with attained education. The median Haitian worker experiences a return of 83, 203, and 1,272 percent for completed primary, secondary, and tertiary[22] education, respectively. For the median worker, however, the returns are slightly lower in rural areas, suggesting that that the heterogeneity of the quality of primary education is a problem. Workers who have completed secondary education face the same problem as those who have completed only primary education. Although returns are significantly higher for completion of one more level of education, the returns vary across the distribution and follow a downward trend. One explanation could be that social networks, or capital that is not captured by some form of unmeasured social capital, may be working better (or may be higher) among the poorer segments than among richer segments of the working population.

Club membership as an indicator of social capital is important in determining wages in rural Haiti, but less so in urban areas. Social capital indicates whether an individual is a member of any popular, peasant, women's, youth, social, sports, cultural, religious, or political organization or club. In the middle-upper part of the income distribution, workers in rural areas obtain returns to social capital of 20 and 24 percent. There are no returns to measurable social capital in urban areas and the lower quintiles in rural areas, except for some social capital that our variable did not capture.

The findings in Table 2.4 show signs of large and measurable inequalities between men and women. Women's incomes are 10 percent higher than men's at the median in urban areas. The picture is somewhat different in rural Haiti, where women are paid less than their male peers.

Poverty

Haiti's per capita GDP performed very poorly in the period 1980–2003, relative to both the country's own historical experience and to other countries in the Latin American and Caribbean region. In 1980 Haiti's per capita GDP stood at $632, and by 2003 it had fallen by about half to $332 (Figure 2.3). In the same period, Jamaica's per capita income increased by around 17 percent, and the Dominican Republic's by 57 percent.[23]

Fundamental to lack of growth in Haiti is the country's long history of political instability, lack of governance, distortions at the macroeconomic level, and inadequate levels of private investment (see Chapters 3 and 4). Macroeconomic stability and a lessening of distortions, so as to encourage private sector investment are essential to increased productivity. More research is needed to determine the exact causes of economic deterioration.

---

22. Very few have tertiary education (only 217 in the whole sample—that is, including non-heads of household).

23. In recent years Haiti's agricultural sector has performed less well than the services and manufacturing sectors. In the 1996–2002 period, agriculture's share of total GDP fell while that of services and industry increased. In 2002, Haiti remained very much a dual economy: on the one hand, agriculture contributed 27.1 percent of GDP and accounted for about 50 percent of employment; on the other, industry contributed 16.3 percent of GDP but accounted for only about 10 percent of jobs. Agricultural output has suffered as a result of a growing population farming a finite land area. The result has been the division of cultivated land into ever smaller plots, such that 78 percent of Haiti's farms were less than two hectares on average by the 1990s.

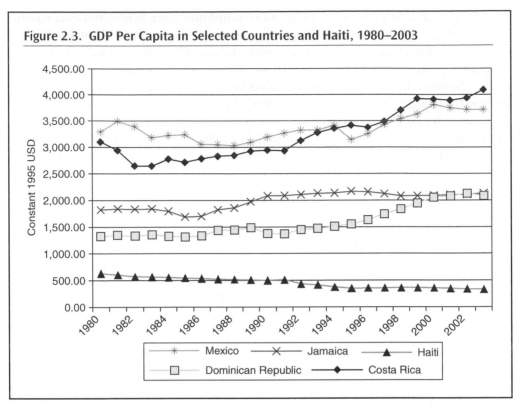

Figure 2.3. GDP Per Capita in Selected Countries and Haiti, 1980–2003

Source: WBI 2004.

Economic growth and a well functioning labor market are important components of a poverty reduction strategy, but they are not the only ones. Programs should ensure that the poor can take advantage of job opportunities, and should protect vulnerable groups that are unable to participate fully in the economy. Information on the poor is needed for these programs to be designed. After the following subsection on income-generation, therefore, the rest addresses headcount poverty and its depth, other poverty indicators, and income inequality.

In 2001, Haiti's extreme poverty for households, measured by P0, was still very high at 49 percent (Figure 2.4).[24] This means that more than 3.9 million people living in extreme poverty. Since the Haiti Living Conditions Survey (HLCS) dataset is the first household survey completed for the country, it is not possible to analyze the extent to which income poverty has changed in the past decade. In the past two decades, GDP per capita (see above) fell dramatically. In conjunction with the information on income inequality presented below, this may indicate that income poverty has increased in recent decades.[25] The

---

24. Appendix C presents the definitions of the different poverty measures. Since the poverty rate is for households, the income (including self-consumption) is for the household. No household reports zero income (including self-consumption); the lowest reported value is of 100 gourdes.

25. More research is needed to address this issue, including per capita income using GNI.

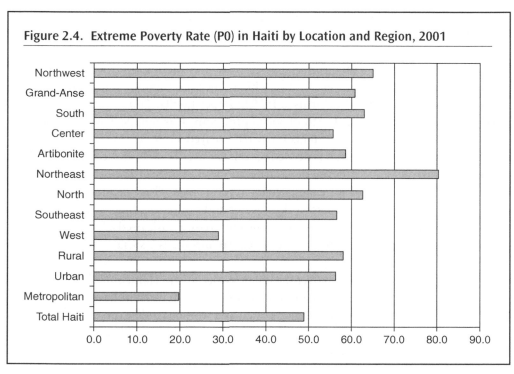

Figure 2.4. Extreme Poverty Rate (P0) in Haiti by Location and Region, 2001

Source: Authors' calculations based on HLCS 2001.

non-monetary indicators, however, reveal that extreme poverty has fallen in the last decade (see below).

There are large differences in headcount poverty among localities and regions in Haiti. Data from 2001 indicate that rural households had the highest rate of extreme poverty: 58 percent were extremely poor in that year (Figure 2.4). Households in the metropolitan area had the lowest extreme poverty rate: 20 percent were extremely poor. Households in other urban areas had a household poverty rate only slightly below that of the rural population: 56 percent were extremely poor. Hence the West region, unsurprisingly, has the lowest extreme poverty rate: 29 percent of households were extremely poor in 2001. The regions with the highest extreme poverty rates are the Northeast and Northwest, where 80 and 65 percent of households, respectively, have a per capita income that takes them below the extreme poverty line of US$1 per day.

The level of poverty in Haiti can also be measured by indicators such as adult illiteracy, infant mortality, and malnutrition; all are very high. In the period 1970–2000, the adult illiteracy rate fell sharply from 78.0 percent to 39.5 percent (EBCM 2000). The greatest improvement was in the 1970–1992 period. The female illiteracy rate, however, has fluctuated. In 2000 and in 1970, fewer males were illiterate (33.4 percent) than females (43.3 percent). Male illiteracy fell throughout the 1970–2000 period. Female illiteracy declined from 82.0 percent in 1970 to 37.9 percent in 1995, but since then the rate has increased, reaching 43.3 percent in 2000. Illiteracy is a major problem in Haiti. Efforts to lower illiteracy are hampered by the fact that many of the illiterates are adults, the result of years of educational neglect. It is more difficult to teach basic skills to adults than to children. Even among young adults, educational performance is poor. The educational deficit, including the question of quality, has a spatial dimension in Haiti. Most of the illiterate aged above 15 years live in rural areas.

The decline in Haiti's infant mortality corroborates the improvement in measured adult illiteracy, although the level is still very high. The infant mortality rate dropped dramatically from 148 per 1,000 live births in 1970 to 79 per 1,000 in 2002.[26] In view of the lack of economic growth and the dearth of social programs, it is not clear what caused this decline. The large volume of remittances may have played a role, as may service provision by NGOs, though more research is needed on this matter. To reduce the infant mortality rate further and reach the Latin American and Caribbean average of 28 per 1,000 live births, a number of measures are required, especially in rural areas. These include general livelihood improvements such as access to clean water and sanitation, high quality education and healthcare, and a daily calorific intake sufficient to cover basic needs. Moreover, Filmer and Pritchett (1997) find that a 10 percent increase in income is associated with a 6 percent lower infant mortality rate.

Life expectancy has increased over the last three decades in Haiti, but it is still very low. As in many parts of Latin America and the Caribbean, men in Haiti have a significantly lower life expectancy than women. In 2002, men and women could expect to live an average of 50 and 54 years, respectively. AIDS is a significant problem in Haiti and, according to the Global Health Council, the large number of AIDS cases has cut average life expectancy by eight years.[27] Were it not for AIDS, therefore, life expectancy would have been 60. Other areas of concern include alcohol and substance use, male violence against women,[28] and general violence.

Haiti has the highest prevalence of HIV/AIDS in the Latin America and the Caribbean (LAC) region and, indeed, the highest incidence outside Africa. The problem has reached epidemic levels, with an estimated 38,000 deaths per year. Women and men are equally affected, mainly through heterosexual transmission. In the 15–49 age group, more than 5 percent are HIV-infected (UNAIDS 2000). The virtual absence of public social protection has further increased the risks for the vulnerable. Contraceptive use is among the lowest in the Western Hemisphere. Teenage pregnancies and HIV/AIDS disproportionately affect youth from low-income families.[29] There are, however, indications that the situation is improving. Haiti was recognized at a recent UN General Assembly Special Session on HIV/AIDS for its progress in improving treatment. It has also been shown that a rapid and effective large-scale AIDS therapy program is possible in Haiti, despite poverty and political unrest (Severe 2005).

Like adult illiteracy and infant mortality, the prevalence of child malnutrition declined in the 1978–2000 period, although it remains very high. Child malnutrition is measured by two

---

26. Infant mortality rate is the number of infants who die before reaching one year of age, per 1,000 live births, in a given year (World Bank 2004).

27. See http://www.globalhealth.org/sources/view.php3?id=668.

28. In fact, results from the household survey surprisingly showed practically no use of or contact with drugs, and levels of alcohol and tobacco use that were not alarmingly high. These results, however, may be explained to some extent by underreporting because of the link to gangs and illegal trade.

29. Moreover, teenage mothers account for 8 percent of all births and contribute to Haiti's high fertility rate.

Table 2.5. Poverty Gaps, 2001

	Metropolitan	Urban	Rural	Total Haiti
P1	8.8	33.4	32.0	26.9
P2	5.2	24.0	22.3	19.3

Source: Calculations based on HLCS 2001. See Appendix C for definition.

variables—weight-for-height and-height-for-age—that fell by about 17 and 20 percentage points, respectively, to 17.3 and 22.7 percent in 2000 (World Bank 2004). Child malnutrition, however, is still significantly higher than the regional LAC average of 9 percent. Efforts to lower the prevalence of child malnutrition are hampered by income poverty and by limited access to quality water, micronutrients, and general healthcare, among other considerations.

Haiti's high poverty incidence can be explained by a series of factors, including as a lack of macroeconomic stability, of good governance, and of political stability. What would happen to extreme poverty rates if Haiti resumed positive economic growth? That matter is addressed in this subsection in the form of uniform economic growth in all sectors.

Poverty Depth and Inequality. Extreme poverty in Haiti is not only extensive but also very deep. The P0 measures the proportion of people below a certain poverty line, but it takes no account of how far they are below that line (the degree of poverty) or whether they are becoming even poorer. To address the situation of the poorest, the squared poverty gap measure, P2, is used.[30] This takes the degree of poverty into account, because it gives more weight to the poorest and most vulnerable. The P2 poverty measure reveals that the extreme poverty depth reached 19.3 percent in 2001 (Table 2.5).

Extreme poverty in rural areas is slightly less deep than in urban Haiti. The P2 measure shows that the extreme poverty depth reached 22 percent in rural areas and 24 percent in urban areas in 2001 (Table 2.5). In the metropolitan area, by contrast, P2 reached only 5 percent in the same year. Haiti's Northeast region has the deepest poverty, and there are significant regional differences. The West region had a P2 of 8.5 but in the Northeast the measure reached 47.4, indicating that poverty is not only widespread but also very deep in the latter region.

Income inequality is part of the reason why Haiti's poverty indicators are worse than in other countries that have similar per capita incomes. Haiti has an extremely unequal income distribution. In 2001, the Gini coefficient for Haiti as a whole was 0.66, above the coefficient for Brazil (0.61). The more unequally income is distributed, the less effective economic growth is in reducing poverty. Income inequality is lower in rural areas (Gini coefficient of 0.59) than in urban (0.67) and metropolitan (0.61) areas in Haiti, and there are wide disparities in the distribution of income across localities and regions.[31] In 2001, the region with the least unequal distribution of per capita income was the Southeast (0.54), while the Northeast had the highest Gini coefficient (0.70).

---

30. See methodology in appendix C.

31. On the basis of expenditure surveys in 1986/1987 and 1999/2000, Pedersen and Lockwood (2001) find that income inequality has increased in the Port-au-Prince area and rural inequality has decreased.

Changes in inequality are typically very slow, except during periods of radical social and institutional change. Where inequality has fallen it has usually happened in association with a substantial expansion and equalization of educational attainment, as in Korea and Malaysia in the 1970s and 1980s. Haiti's expansion in education (a reduction in educational inequalities) has thus far been too small to have a significant effect on skills composition.

Poverty Correlates: Does Rural Poverty Differ from Urban Poverty?

After counting the extreme poor above, it is important to know who they are, the character of their poverty, where they live, and what they do. Comparing average levels of poverty for different categories is useful for learning which population groups are falling behind or catching up in terms of poverty. This is helpful in designing policies: we would like to know, for example, not only whether more or less educated people are more likely to be poor in Haiti, but also how the likelihood of being poor compares among rural and urban areas, as well as among the nine regions. This section addresses poverty on the basis of P0 for various population groups in 2001. The main questions are: (1) Who are the poor? (2) What are the characteristics of poor households? (3) Where do they live? (4) Where do they work?

This section analyzes the relative importance of some of these and other correlates of rural and urban poverty in a multivariate setting. It also investigates the marginal impact of each attribute on the likelihood of a household's falling below the indigence poverty line, taking other characteristics into account. The section examines the impact of experience, labor market association, different levels of education, and so forth on the likelihood of being poor for rural areas and for Haiti as a whole.[32] Because of the way the regression model is specified, the findings show when the impacts for rural areas are different from those for Haiti as a whole.

The analysis of poverty correlates reveals a conditional correlation between poverty and the characteristics of household heads, and also indicates groups that are particularly vulnerable. Analysis of the probability of a household's being poor reveals that disparities in assets such as education are indeed strongly correlated with poverty.

Rural living is in many ways very different from urban and metropolitan living in Haiti (see Table D.4). Residence in rural areas does not in itself affect the probability of being poor. Individual and household characteristics are more important than geographic location. This is good news for policy-makers, since there are no nonmeasurable rural variables affecting the likelihood of a rural household's falling below the extreme poverty line.

---

32. The status of the household (poor or nonpoor) is regressed on relevant individual and household characteristics using the probit regression technique. Standard errors are adjusted for the clustering process inherent in the sampling procedure of the HCLS survey. It is important to note the limitations of this analysis at the outset. First and foremost, the analysis does not capture the dynamic impact of certain causes of poverty over time. Most notably, the impact of changes in economic growth—most certainly a key determinant of poverty—cannot be assessed using this static, cross-section model. Second, the analysis is limited by the variables available at the household level from the 2001 HLCS. Other factors—physical conditions such as variations in climate or access to markets—could not be included because of a lack of data at this level. Finally, though theory holds that many of the variables included in the analysis do indeed contribute to (cause) poverty (or poverty reduction), the statistical relationships should be interpreted as correlates and not as determinants, since causality can run both ways for some variables.

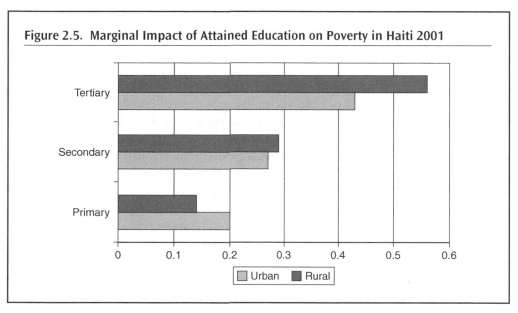

Figure 2.5. Marginal Impact of Attained Education on Poverty in Haiti 2001

Source: Authors' calculations based on HLCS 2001.

The gender of heads of household and social capital affect poverty in rural areas but not in others. Households headed by women in rural Haiti are 11 percent more likely to be poor than those headed by men, when other covariates (such as labor market connection and education) are included in the analysis (Table D.4). Hence the need for social policies that favor women, such as conditional cash transfer programs like the *Bolsa Família* initiative in Brazil, whereby the mother receives the benefit. Membership of a club as an indicator of social capital appears to be important to escaping poverty in rural areas. The analysis shows that rural dwellers with little or no social capital have a higher incidence of poverty than their peers who do have social capital, controlling for other characteristics (Table D.4). It is interesting to note that social capital has no measurable poverty-reducing effect in urban areas, as also shown in the income determination analysis above.

As in the income generation analysis, education is the strongest poverty reduction correlate in Haiti. All levels of education from primary to tertiary are strongly and statistically significant, and are negatively associated with the probability of being poor (Table D.4 and Figure 2.5). The more education a household head attains, the less likely it is that he or she will have fallen below the poverty line of US$1 a day in 2001. Note that the likelihood of falling below the poverty line is higher for primary school graduates in rural areas than in other areas, which indicates that primary education is less effective in reducing poverty. Another explanation could be that the quality of primary education may not be as high in rural areas as in urban or metropolitan areas.

The bigger a household, the higher its probability of being extremely poor. Family characteristics such as household size are positively correlated with the incidence of extreme poverty. Thus, the larger a household is, the more poverty-prone it is (see Table D.4).[33]

---

33. Moreover, larger households are poorer and the effect is concave, indicating that a scaling factor matters for poverty.

Migration status is a significant correlate to poverty: migrants have an 8 percent lower probability of falling into extreme poverty than their peers who never migrated. Households that migrated to the metropolitan from rural areas show the same reduced risk of falling into poverty as those households that migrated from other areas (see Table D.4).

The structure of poverty in Haiti is clear (controlling for individual and household characteristics, location, and region): residence in rural areas does not in itself affect the probability of being poor; female-headed households in rural areas are more likely to experience poverty than male-headed households; young households/household heads are more likely to be poor than older households/household heads; and those engaged in agriculture are not more likely to experience poverty than those engaged in services and industry. Poverty, therefore, is by no means strictly an agricultural problem. It is slightly more extensive in urban areas than in rural areas. Poverty and low levels of education are broadly correlated but the less educated in rural areas are more likely to be poor than their urban peers. Social capital protects against poverty in rural areas but the impact is not statistically significant in urban areas. Migration and education are two other factors that reduce the likelihood of falling into poverty. Without interventions to improve poor people's opportunities and assets, their plight is likely to worsen.

Simulation of the Effect of Economic Growth on Poverty in Haiti

Simulations of uniform growth in all sectors reveal that the immediate impact on poverty reduction is relatively small for low positive annual growth rates. The key instrument for poverty reduction through job creation is growth. But growth alone will not produce sufficient gains in poverty reduction in the short to medium term, because real economic growth has been negative in recent years and income is unequally distributed (see above). For example, simple simulation exercises show that if income per capita in Haiti as a whole grew by 2 percent per year from 2001, the rates of extreme poverty would fall by only 3.3 percentage points after five years (Table 2.7). After 10 years, the gains would be greater, but the rate of extreme poverty would still be high at 42.2 percent. Even if the country were able to generate a record high growth rate, resulting in a 5 or 10 percent growth in per capita income, this would have to be sustained for 10 years to bring the extreme poverty rates down to 33.5 and 22.9 percent, respectively. The projected poverty impact of increased uniform economic growth is much greater in metropolitan areas than in other urban and rural areas. After 10 years of steady real economic growth of 2 percent annually, extreme poverty falls by roughly 18 percent in the metropolitan areas, and by 11 and 14 percent in urban and rural areas, respectively. The same pattern holds true for larger annual growth rates. One explanation is that poverty in Haiti is not only broad but also deep, as indicated above. More research is needed to address propoor growth in Haiti.

All the simulations presented in this section were based on a series of assumptions, including the supposition that per capita income grows equally in Haiti. But this is unlikely to be the case: the literature on other countries shows that income grows very unequally for different income groups. For the findings in this section, this means that the estimated poverty reduction impacts are much smaller than stated because poor households will benefit much less than rich households. Hence the need for much broader policies than economic growth strategies if poverty in Haiti is to be significantly reduced.

Table 2.7. Projected Poverty Reduction Impact of Uniform Growth in Haiti

	Years	Estimated Poverty Rate (P0)			
		Total	Metro	Urban	Rural
P0 in 2001		48.9	19.7	56.3	58.1
2% real annual per capita growth	1	48.2	19.3	56.0	57.2
	5	45.6	17.8	53.3	54.1
	10	42.2	16.1	49.9	50.1
5% real annual per capita growth	1	47.3	19.1	55.0	56.0
	5	41.1	15.7	48.8	48.7
	10	33.5	10.7	41.6	40.0
10% real annual per capita growth	1	45.7	17.9	53.5	54.3
	5	33.9	10.8	42.1	40.4
	10	22.9	5.7	30.2	27.5

Note: P0 for households (not individuals), based on total per capita income including self-consumption.
Source: Authors' calculations based on HLCS 2001.

Migration

Poorer regions and those with fewer economic opportunities have traditionally sent migrants to more prosperous regions. The West region, where economic conditions are most favorable, has historically received migrants. Both sending and receiving regions may benefit from migration. The West benefits by importing skilled and unskilled labor, which makes local capital more productive. The sending regions benefit from upward pressures on wages and from remittances that migrant households return to their region of origin (which may outweigh the cost of the brain drain). Nonetheless, migration may also have negative impacts on the sending region as a result of the brain drain and the disruption of social capital.

There are various reasons for the changing demographic pattern, and many of them relate to economic opportunities. It is clear, for example, that living conditions in the rural Northeast are inferior to those in the West. Rural areas in the West are close to Port-au-Prince, and the rural population therefore has easy access to goods and services that are produced, imported, or provided by the capital. Moreover, rural farmers in the West have easier access to a large market for their produce than do other regions such as the Northeast, because roads and other infrastructure are limited in the poor regions.

Migration is a coping mechanism for youth and for the population generally in the face of unemployment, poverty, and lack of opportunities. In Haiti, more than one in five people aged 15 or more were not born in the region where they now live.

Migration is directed overwhelmingly toward the metropolitan area, where 51 percent of current residents were born in other parts of the country.[34] Nearly 17 percent of all

---

34. Among adults above 14 years of age, only 35 percent of the current metropolitan area residents were born in that area.

Table 2.8. Domestic Migration, 2001 (percent)

	Migrated	Not Migrated
Artibonite	7.6	92.4
Center	15.3	84.7
Grand-Anse	11.5	88.5
North	4.9	95.1
Northeast	23.6	76.4
Northwest	1.9	98.1
West	36.7	63.3
South	11.2	88.8
Southeast	8.3	91.7
Total	20.4	79.6

Source: Authors' calculations based on HLCS 2001.

Haitians over the age of 18 have migrated at some point to Port-au-Prince. Twelve percent of the area's adult population moved into the metropolitan region in the past five years.

In the most populous region, the West, 36.7 percent of the population was born elsewhere in Haiti (Table 2.8). Those who migrate are mainly economic migrants. Data show that migrants aged 15 and above who left a specific region have higher average years of schooling than those who stayed behind.[35] Only the few who left the metropolitan area are less educated than their peers, but their level of education is still higher than the average in other regions, and thus migration gives them a competitive advantage. On average, migrants have nearly three more years of completed education than nonmigrants.

A variety of factors help explain migration, because not all migration is based on direct self-selection. It is somewhat surprising that most domestic migrants are women. The main reason why Haitians migrate is that they follow their families (Table 2.9).

Table 2.9. Reason for Migration, Youth and Adults, 2001 (percent)

Followed family	36.5
Educational reasons	13.0
Personal reasons	11.7
Lack of work	9.4
Other (including work)	29.4

Source: Authors' calculations based on HLCS 2001.

Positive self-selection implies that migration generally tends to improve the financial situation of the migrant's household.[36] Analysis of the household survey data (Table 2.15 below) supports the proposition that youth who migrate are, ceteris paribus, less likely to be unemployed or inactive than those who stay in their region of origin.

There are few opportunities in many rural and urban areas. What is the likelihood that someone will migrate to Port-au-Prince from elsewhere in the country, and who is more or less likely to migrate? Port-au-Prince, despite its scarcity of formal jobs, attracts people from other areas, especially urban areas. The data in Table 2.10 show that many people from rural areas are less likely to migrate to Port-au-Prince than their urban peers.[37] The more educated are also

---

35. The data did not allow an examination of age at the time of migration, so it has not been possible to calculate the proportion migrating as youth.

36. This does not necessarily mean that they are better off than average in the new place of residence.

37. Urban here means other all urban areas other than Port-au-Prince.

far more likely than the less educated to be migrants: tertiary school graduates are almost 40 percent more likely to migrate than primary school graduates, who are 5 percent more likely to leave than their peers with no completed education.

International migration has affected Haiti for at least four decades. The net migration rate (2.3 per 1,000 Haitians—Table 2.11) has been higher than the population growth rate (2.2 percent) since at least 1985. There are more than 75,000 Haitians or persons of Haitian origin in the Bahamas, 500,000 in the Dominican Republic, and 2 million in the United States. As many as 30 percent of all Haitian households, and 44 percent of metropolitan households, have "close relatives" abroad.[38] Overall, the vast majority (72 percent) of these relatives live in high-income countries such as the United States and Canada.

Large-scale emigration from Haiti began in the late 1950s. At first, those leaving were seeking a better standard

Table 2.10. Likelihood of Migrating to Port-au-Prince, 2001

Migrated	dF/dX	Z
Age	0.00	−2.33
Female*	0.01	1.60
Family size	−0.01	−2.64
Squared family size	0.00	1.39
Primary education*	0.05	6.80
Secondary education*	0.13	12.69
Tertiary education*	0.45	9.43
Industry*	0.13	5.72
Agriculture*	−0.14	−10.14
Service*	0.05	3.29
Inactive*	0.01	0.74
Rural*	−0.31	−39.03

Note: Probit regression, reporting marginal effects. Pseudo R2 = 0.417. Includes people living in Port-au-Prince but not born there and people living outside Port-au-Prince in their region of birth. Conditioned on being at least 18 years old. Number of observations: 13,158. Omitted variables: no education completed and public sector.

Source: Authors' calculation based on HLCS 2001.

of living abroad and were technicians, skilled workers, and business leaders who left mainly for sociopolitical reasons. During the 1960s, semi-skilled Haitian professionals joined the exodus for economic and political reasons, and increasingly headed to the United States. The flow continued during the 1980s, mainly comprising nontechnicians who also left for economic and political reasons. A new phase of emigration from Haiti to the United States began in 1972 and continues in the form of sailboats carrying Haitians to the Bahamas, Jamaica, and the United States. Participants in this new phase of emigration were more likely to be poorer Haitians who could not afford exit visas or airplane tickets but who could, by selling their possessions or land, raise the amount charged by boat captains. Most of these migrants came from outside Port-au-Prince.

Members of the Haitian diaspora send cash transfers and other resources back to Haiti, which has been identified as the world's most remittance-dependent country. It is hard to estimate the exact amount of remittances to Haiti because of poor statistical information and informal channels of exchange, but the estimates currently available suggest that expatriates send home about US$700–900 million per year—about a quarter of the country's

---

38. In the HLCS 2001, "close relatives" are defined as parents, spouses, children, or siblings.

Table 2.11. Migration from Haiti, 1985–2005

	1985–1990	1990–1995	1995–2000	2000–2005
Net migration (per 1000)	2.8	3.4	2.6	2.3

Source: IHSI 2003.

GDP and about three times higher than the foreign aid Haiti receives annually.[39] Financial transfers (remittances) from the diaspora constitute the most important private risk management and social protection system for Haitian households. The 1999–2000 expenditure survey[40] reveals that 40 percent of Haitian households receive transfers either from resident households (21.9 percent) or from expatriate households (11.9 percent) or both at the same time (5.7 percent). In 2004, the total amount of transfers (internal and external) was estimated at more than US$1 billion, 80 percent of which came from Haitians living abroad. There are disparities, however, in the distribution of these remittances. Sixty-eight percent of households in Port-au-Prince and 41 percent of households in rural and other urban areas receive transfers from abroad.[41] Transfers make up 31 percent of the average revenue of households in Port-au-Prince and other urban areas, and 16 percent of the average revenue of rural households.[42] Remittances average US$180 per household per year, although the range is wide.[43] Together with humanitarian food aid, these remittances constitute the main social safety net in Haiti.

Many Haitians living abroad return regularly, for example for carnival and vacations. Although Haiti is still predominantly a society of peasant farmers, it is changing. The very slow improvements in telecommunications and urbanization are creating a population that is more closely linked to the global system. Moreover, Haitian expatriates conduct a large variety of micro-level and charitable activities in their towns and villages of origin. These activities span small public work projects, school canteens, school programs, health clinics, and library construction. Although these activities contribute greatly to social development, they do not make a significant contribution to the economic growth of the localities they serve. The challenges facing Haiti today are multiple and multidimensional, and meeting them requires a critical mass of educated people. Haitian expatriates, therefore, are not only important because they have projects in towns and villages, and send back remittances, but because Haiti's future development is dependent on their human capital.

Remittances are an important part of many families' income, but emigration also causes a lack of qualified workers or a brain drain in Haiti. Very few return migrants are

---

39. The value is in 1995 dollars.
40. L'enquête budget consommation des ménages, EBCM.
41. HLCS 2001.
42. HLCS 2001.
43. HLCS 2001.

observed in the 2001 household survey. For youth, the lack of parental role models (particularly fathers) caused by emigration leaves an even bigger gap. Migration may lead to stressful situations for children and youth left behind with only one parent, with another family member, or with friends. The migration of parents thus increases the risk that small children and youth will be neglected.

Endowment and Distribution Of Assets And Resources

The problem of poverty and inequality in Haiti largely reflects disparities in opportunities. The distribution of key productive assets—labor, human capital, physical assets, financial assets, and social capital—is highly unequal. These disparities are greatest between the poor and nonpoor, but they also manifest themselves differently by geographic region. Additionally, access to services is unequal. This section addresses several of these areas: education, basic infrastructure services, and social assistance. It then looks at employment, unemployment and coping strategies, before ending with an analysis of social cohesion and violence. The importance of education and other assets for employment, and in determining wages and income, are addressed in the subsection below.

The value of the goods produced by the population is closely linked to skills and other human and social capital, as well as to the availability of infrastructure and other physical capital, as discussed in this section. With greater human and social capital, production capacity and product quality increase and production value improves, as do the population's household incomes. Rural household income also increases with access to better irrigation systems, flood control, energy, and good roads.

Human Capital

Education is essential for poverty reduction. Increased educational attainment can improve the livelihoods of the poor and reduce the likelihood of becoming poor. More education is also a key factor in obtaining a higher income, and education reduces the fertility rate (see above). One clear message, therefore, is that Haitians would greatly benefit from being helped to move up the educational ladder.

Haiti underinvests in human capital and the quality of education is alarmingly low (World Bank 1998). An indicator of poor quality is the low internal efficiency in primary and secondary education, and the resulting high proportion of overage students. In order to bring Haitians up the educational ladder, it is essential to provide for basic human needs and human capital accumulation. Investments in the education, health, and nutritional status of the population contribute to a productive labor force, better living conditions, and higher per capita income. It should be noted, however, that the government faces serious budgetary constraints on investments in all sectors, including education (see Chapter 3).

Educational disparity is three-pronged in Haiti—across age, location, and income. The level of educational attainment of the adult and youth population varies by location. Educational attainment for household heads increased steadily each decade from 1930 to 1980 (Figure 2.6).

Youth and adults living in rural areas have accumulated far less human capital than their peers in urban areas, perhaps in part because the most educated leave rural areas.

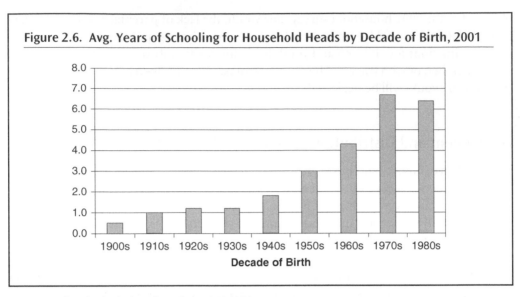

Figure 2.6. Avg. Years of Schooling for Household Heads by Decade of Birth, 2001

Source: Authors' calculations based on HLCS 2001.

Efforts are needed to improve the poor's access to basic, quality education. There is an enormous variation among the different age groups. Of young children (five year-olds) only 4.3 percent receive formal education (preschool, for example); see Table 2.12. Some 77 percent of those between the ages of 6 and 11 receive formal education, and the attendance rate increases to 81.5 percent for children between the ages of 12 and 14. Location matters for school attendance. Youth and adults in rural areas have accumulated far less human capital than their urban peers. In part this might be because the most educated leave rural areas. In the metropolitan area, 82.1 percent of those between the ages of 6 and 11 attend school. In urban areas, 84.8 percent of this age group attend school, but the number falls to 73.3 percent in rural areas. Moreover, travel time to school is often long for children in rural areas, especially poor children who have to walk. Of youth aged 18 to 24, only 39.1 percent attend formal education, but the variation across locations is wide. Some

Table 2.12. School Attendance by Age, 2001 (percent)

Age	Metro	Urban	Rural	Total Haiti
5	4.7	5.7	3.8	4.3
6–11	82.1	84.8	73.3	77.0
12–14	84.6	87.0	78.6	81.5
15–17	79.3	79.9	71.3	74.8
18–24	46.6	44.1	32.8	39.1

Source: Authors' calculations based on HLCS 2001.

Table 2.13. School Attendance of 7–14 Year-Olds by Income Quintile (percent), 2001

Quintile	Metro	Urban	Rural	Total Haiti
1 (poorest)	73.7	78.5	71.2	73.6
2	80.8	89.0	73.8	77.1
3	90.9	84.6	78.1	78.6
4	88.7	90.7	77.4	82.7
5 (richest)	86.1	89.8	85.2	87.2

Source: Authors' calculations based on HLCS 2001.

46.6 percent of this age group are in school in the metropolitan area, compared to only 32.8 percent in rural areas.[44]

There are large gaps in school attendance between the poor and nonpoor. Attendance is unequal across income quintiles. As Table 2.12 shows, the trend is rapidly increasing for successively higher income quintiles, indicating the regressive nature of benefit incidence in education. Some 74 percent of the poorest (first quintile) receive primary school services, while 87 percent of the richest (fifth quintile) do so. The school attendance of extremely poor students still lags in Haiti. This is true in all three locations, and urban children from extremely poor families (the two lowest quintiles) lag slightly less than the extremely poor in other locations—in the second urban quintile, attendance as high as 89 percent (Table 2.13).

School fees represent a large part of family income—between 15 and 25 percent of average household annual income per child for the poorest 20 percent of households, and between 5 and 6 percent in rural areas. A recent report by Médecins Sans Frontières found that nearly half of all families who pay for health services do so by resorting to nonsustainable coping strategies such as selling their assets (Médecins Sans Frontières 2005). It also found that these strategies are more common among the poorest families.

Education also seems to reduce the risk of falling into poverty in Haiti (see above). Policies to improve the poor's access to primary and secondary education, linked to improved educational quality and a sharper focus on technical skills, should be the core of the country's poverty reduction strategy.

Access to Basic Infrastructure Services

Basic infrastructure services contribute to greater well-being and productivity. Some services, such as potable water and sanitation, make a direct contribution to overall well-being and health status. Others, such as electricity and telephones, help households use their

---

44. There are also wide differences in school attendance across regions, whereby children and youths in the poorest regions fall behind their peers in the richer areas. For example, in the Northwest and Artibonite, 71.3 and 68.1 percent of 6–11 year-olds attended school in 2001, compared to 80.3 and 78.7 percent in the West and Center regions.

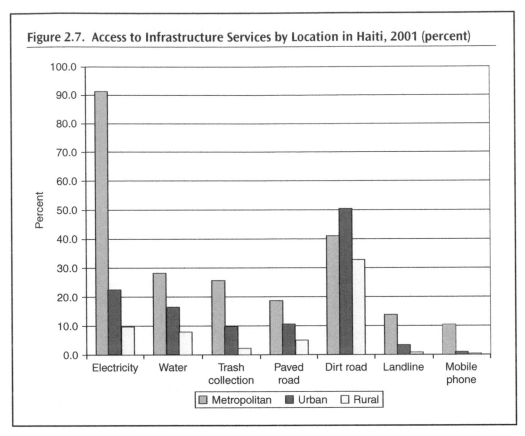

Figure 2.7. Access to Infrastructure Services by Location in Haiti, 2001 (percent)

Source: Authors' calculations based on HLCS 2001.

homes productively in order to generate income. Research shows that access to basic services is highly correlated with a lower probability of being poor. Inequities in access to such services abound in Haiti's rural and urban areas, both between the poor and nonpoor and by geographical area. Key gaps for the rural poor include potable water, energy, and roads. The impact of corruption on service delivery is addressed in Chapter 3. There is evidence that corruption and the misuse of public funds have lowered the quality and coverage of all public services (World Bank 1998).

Access to public infrastructure services is generally poor in Haiti, especially in rural areas, and the rural-metropolitan gap is wide. In the public sector, only 20 percent of resources go to rural areas, where most people live (World Bank 1998). Haiti's rural population has little access to safe water; only 7.9 percent have access to water supplied by a public or private company, compared to 28 percent in the metropolitan area (Figure 2.7). Rural dwellers have less access to safe water than some of their peers in rural African countries such as Kenya (31 percent) and Uganda (46 percent) (UNICEF 2000).

The incidence of water access varies among rich and poor households. As Figure 2.8 shows, the trend is increasing for successively higher income quintiles. In rural and urban areas, the first quintile in the income distribution receives less than 4 and 9 percent, respectively, of water services, while the fifth quintile receives more than 10 and 29 percent, respectively. The benefit incidence of water is concentrated in the fifth quintile in all locations.

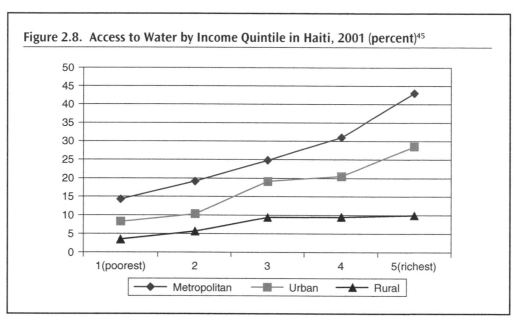

Figure 2.8. Access to Water by Income Quintile in Haiti, 2001 (percent)[45]

Source: Authors' calculations based on HLCS 2001.

There are significant differences in access to energy. Households in the metropolitan area have far more access than those elsewhere. Energy and electrification projects help improve living conditions. The supply facilitates social integration, helps increase production value, and promotes diversification. As regards energy sources for cooking, rural residents mainly use charcoal while urban dwellers use propane, which entail both health and safety risks. Different localities have disparate levels of access to the electrical network. Only 9.8 percent of rural households have access to electricity, compared to 91.4 percent of households in the metropolitan area (Figure 2.7).

There are also very wide differences across the income distribution in access to electricity (Figure 2.9). The general trend is one of increasing access for successively higher income quintiles, which indicates the regressive nature of electrification in urban and rural areas. In metropolitan Haiti there is a high and fairly equal access to electricity across the income distribution.

Because the provision of drinking water, sewerage networks, and electricity to a dispersed rural population would be very costly, efforts should first target the agglomerated population in localities, regions, and provinces with the most acute level and highest density of poverty. Special programs should also be devised with appropriate technologies to improve the rural population's access to water.

There are wide differences in access to roads. Households in rural areas lag behind those in urban areas. Only 5 and 33 percent of the rural population have access to paved

45. Quintiles are within area. A direct comparison of deciles in the graph does not reflect two groups with the same average income but rather the same proportion of people—thus ensuring, for example, that the first decile is not composed mainly of people from rural areas and a few from the metropolitan area.

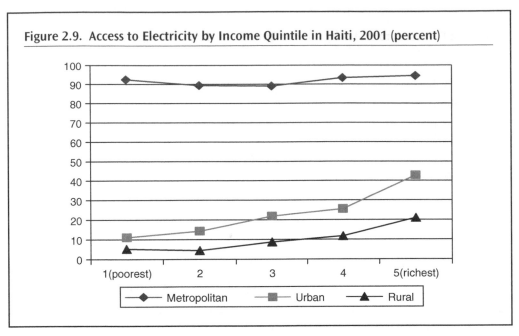

Figure 2.9. Access to Electricity by Income Quintile in Haiti, 2001 (percent)

Source: Authors' calculations based on HLCS 2001.

and dirt roads, respectively (Figure 2.7). Of the urban population, 11 and 50 percent, respectively, have access to paved and dirt roads. Roads play multiple roles associated with poverty alleviation and the improvement of the poor rural population's quality of life. They are essential elements for the production and marketing of products, stimulating economic activity that results in greater job opportunities and better income levels. They also facilitate access to labor markets and allow greater labor participation by the rural population in nonagricultural activities outside rural areas. In addition, they help improve quality of life by facilitating communication and access to basic services such as health or education, enabling greater social participation by more distant sectors.

The general trend is increased access to roads for successively higher income quintiles. Rural households have little access, regardless of location in the income distribution, indicating no clear regressive nature of road access in rural areas (Figure 2.10).

Access to safe water supplied by a public or private company is a major problem in Haiti, and access to electricity is the most unequal among locations. Most of the urban population has access to electricity, compared to only 10 percent of the rural population. Moreover, only about 8 percent of Haitians have access to a paved road and 3 percent have a telephone. Finally, the extremely poor have much less access to services than their non-poor peers.

Employment

It seems clear that the economy must remain a focal point for policy-makers seeking to improve livelihoods. In 2002, Haiti remained very much a dual economy in which agriculture

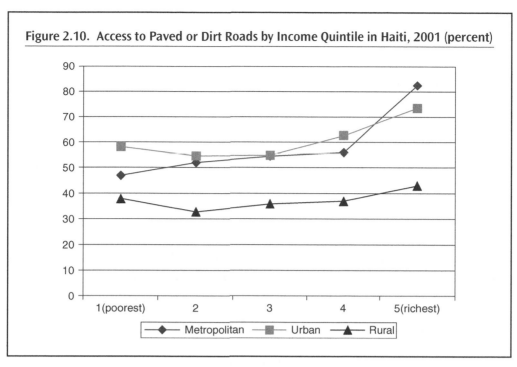

Figure 2.10. Access to Paved or Dirt Roads by Income Quintile in Haiti, 2001 (percent)

Source: Authors' calculations based on HLCS 2001.

contributes 27.1 percent of GDP and accounts for about 50 percent of employment, while industry contributes 16.3 percent of GDP, but accounts for only about 10 percent of jobs. Employment is therefore essential, and both the farm and nonfarm sectors play a crucial role. The labor market in Haiti is dual; one for men and one for women. Most men work in agriculture but few employed women do (Table 2.14). In contrast, most employed women work in the service sector, but few men do.[46]

Labor markets are important for improving livelihoods and for reducing poverty in Haiti. Employment is essential to lifting poor families out of poverty. Haiti's population growth will slow down over the longer term, which will affect poverty through its broader effects on the labor market. The population growth of previous decades has resulted in an elastic supply of unskilled labor. As a result, wage levels have remained low except for a few highly skilled, well educated workers who are employed, for example, in banking, car dealing, or pharmaceuticals.

Labor is poor people's most abundant asset and it accounts for most of their total income (see above). Nonetheless, the poor are constrained in their labor use in several ways: lack of jobs, low wages, and wage discrimination, especially for women. The poverty

---

46. This pattern is unchanged as age increases. In view of the difference in the proportion of young males and females attending school, as well as the duality of the labor market, more research on gender issues is needed.

Table 2.14. Work Sector by Gender 2001 (percent)

	Male				Female			
Age	Agriculture	Industry	Service	Public	Agriculture	Industry	Service	Public
15–19	76.8	11.7	11.5	0.0	32.1	3.7	61.8	2.4
20–24	57.0	16.8	19.3	6.9	23.7	7.1	66.3	3.0
25–34	43.3	19.3	23.3	14.1	16.8	6.1	68.1	9.1
35–44	54.2	13.7	24.4	7.7	21.4	5.2	65.3	8.1

Source: Authors' calculations based on HLCS 2001.

analysis below reveals that many Haitian workers are poor despite working full time, and thus it is important that the quality of jobs, as well as their quantity, is raised. The challenge of job creation, therefore, is to increase worker productivity and tighten the labor market for competitive wages, so as to lift the employee's household out of poverty. This section addresses employment and unemployment. Income sources and income generation are addressed below.

Migration and remittances have led to an expansion in areas such as home-building and banking, which has created work for construction and business workers, but most new entrants into the labor market join the estimated one million Haitians in the informal sector who are engaged in a multitude of occupations, from self-employed traders and artisans to casual laborers. One of the most common activities is the reselling of minute quantities of everyday goods and basic services. Markets and streets are full of people attempting to make a living by selling items such as used clothing, fruit and vegetables, chewing gum, pens, and soap. Others run roadside microenterprises that repair broken machinery, or break rocks for use in house or road construction. These are classic coping strategies in Haiti. Most Haitians in rural areas are always working—weeding fields, harvesting crops, fetching drinking water, or driving livestock to fresh pasture. They receive fewer remittances than their urban peers and cannot afford to be idle.

Formal sector jobs are few. Ninety percent of the formal economy jobs are in Port-au-Prince. About half of formal jobs are in the public sector, particularly in education, health, and justice. Others jobs are in state-owned enterprises such as telephone and electricity companies, or in the police force and the tax and customs services. The rest of those with formal employment work in the small private sector, mainly in assembly factories, banking, commerce, and transportation. Since 1995, the one area of employment that has increased sharply is the provision of private security, reflecting concerns about increased crime (see below).

Unemployment and underemployment are at critical levels, particularly in urban areas. The unemployment rate reached 23.5 percent in 2001, according to the household survey. The rate is highest in urban areas: 38.9 and 19.4 percent in metropolitan and other urban areas, respectively, compared to 17.5 percent in rural areas.

Agricultural and Nonagricultural Employment. The nonfarm sector is heterogeneous and includes a wide variety of activities and productivity levels across nonfarm jobs. The sector can reduce poverty in several distinct but qualitatively important ways. First, high-productivity activities seem to provide the population with sufficient income to escape poverty. Second, vulnerable segments of the population, such as the poorest, tend to be concentrated in low or less productive rural nonagricultural activities, mainly because of skill and educational deficiencies and location disadvantages. These low-productivity/return occupations nevertheless make a critical contribution to livelihoods and prevent further destitution.

Recent research in developing countries shows that the nonfarm sector plays a positive role in absorbing a growing rural labor force and in slowing rural-urban migration. Moreover, the nonagricultural sector contributes to national income growth and helps promote more equitable income distribution (Lanjouw and Lanjouw 2001). Lanjouw and Lanjouw also find that the nonagricultural sector is large and growing in developing countries. In Latin America alone, 47 percent of the labor force in rural settlements and rural towns is employed in off-farm activities. Some 79 percent of women in the Latin American rural labor force are employed off-farm. Haiti is only slightly different from the LAC region in this regard: 52.4 percent of workers are engaged off-farm—98.7, 55.4, and 37.2 percent in metropolitan, urban, and rural areas, respectively, in 2001.

What determines the types of workers most likely to seek employment in and outside the agricultural sector? Table E.1 presents the findings of three models linking the probability of a worker having primary employment in a nonagricultural wage labor occupation to a range of explanatory variables. The first model comprises all combined nonfarm activities in Haiti, the second and third models split those employed in the nonagricultural labor force into two groups: those with a low-productivity (low-return) job and those with a high-productivity (high-return) job.

Considering all nonfarm employment together, women are significantly more represented in the nonagricultural wage labor force than men (Table E.3).[47] The difference between male and female participation rates is leveling out in the high-productivity nonfarm sector. In rural areas the latter findings are even stronger: women tend to be much more engaged off-farm than men. Moreover, the effect of education is strong.

With regard to the uneducated, those with at least one level of completed education are generally more likely to find employment in the nonagricultural sector. As educational attainment rises, so does the probability of employment in the nonagricultural sector. Completion of primary education raises the probability of employment in high-return jobs to around 21 percent. Spatial heterogeneity is wide: geography influences the probabilities of nonfarm sector participation. Relative to those living in the West region, workers living in the other eight regions are less likely to be employed in highly productive nonagricultural sectors and in nonagricultural sectors generally.

---

47. This finding is similar to that for poor northeastern Brazil, where women are also more likely to be represented in the agricultural sector (Ferreira and Lanjouw 2001).

Rural residents outside the West and Center regions are significantly less likely than those in the rural West region to be employed in nonagricultural activities. Hence workers in rural localities are not confined solely to cultivation, since wage employment opportunities do exist. An improvement in transport infrastructure, which provides access to urban centers, may facilitate access to off-farm jobs.

Migration status also affects the sector of employment. Workers who migrated have a higher likelihood of being employed in the nonfarm sector, and a slightly higher likelihood of working in the high-productivity nonfarm sector than those who stay in the specific rural area.

Analysis of correlates of nonfarm employment in Haiti suggests that the four key determinants of access to employment and productivity in nonfarm activities are education, gender, location, and migration status. This finding is underscored when nonfarm activities are divided into low-return and high-return activities. There is evidence that the nonfarm sectors are more vibrant in more populated areas, which are connected to markets and have certain minimum standards of infrastructure. Government and donors should therefore help increase the rural population's access to infrastructure services and human capital, so that it can take advantage of increased opportunities.

Unemployment

Haiti has about 1.6 million youth (aged 15 to 24). In the West region, youth constitute 23 percent of the population. In fact, the West region is home to more than 45 percent of Haiti's entire youth population. The least youth-populous regions, such as the Northeast and Southeast, are home to only 3 and 4 percent, respectively, of the country's youth population.

Nearly half of Haitian youth are not enrolled in school and 47.4 percent of those participating in the labor market are unemployed, the highest proportion in LAC. One way of coping with unemployment and the lack of opportunities is for youth to migrate, either abroad or to another region or town in Haiti.

It is very difficult to penetrate the labor market and find a job in Haiti; finding a good job is even harder. Practically everyone finds unemployment to be a serious problem, and more than two out of three youth find it to be a *very* serious problem. Eight out of ten youth attend school at age 13, about one in two at age 19, and fewer than one in five at age 24. Those who leave school enter the labor market or become inactive because of illness, teenage pregnancy, household work, involvement in illegal activities, or other reasons. The proportion of those unemployed and inactive is between an astonishing 45 and 55 percent for the 20–30 age group, while the proportion of those who are inactive is 20 percent in the 35–44 age group. Clearly, unemployment is a problem that affects youth disproportionately, since the unemployment rate drops markedly to 34.5 and 20.2 percent for age groups 25–34 and 35–44, respectively. Unemployment is not transient or seasonal: three-quarters of the unemployed report that they have never had a job.

A multivariate analysis reveals that women are, ceteris paribus, more likely to be unemployed than men (Table 2.15) and more likely to leave school earlier than men. Religious affiliation also affects the probability of being unemployed. Catholics and Voodooists are more likely than their peers to leave school but less likely to be unemployed. For this group, therefore, a reason for leaving school at an early age may be the greater availability of jobs.[49] Marriage appears to drive youth out of school and into employment. Because the model does not account for the quality of jobs, it may be a cause for concern that the positive correlation stems from the fact that married youth are indirectly forced to accept any job available in order to provide for their dependents. On the other hand, family economics generally suggest that married people have better traits than their peers and would therefore be more likely to find (good) jobs. Finally, migrants are less likely to be unemployed than nonmigrants (see Table 2.15).

Social Cohesion and Violence

Especially in fragile states, the ability of communities and households to work and live together by establishing bonds of mutual trust, as well as to penalize wrongdoing, are essential to maintaining people's livelihoods, security, and welfare. Such aspects of community cohesion, or social capital, are difficult to measure, but a number of

Table 2.15. Probability of Youth being Unemployed or Inactive 2001[48]

Unemployed/Inactive	Coefficient	t
Age	−0.377	−2.24
Age squared	0.007	1.70
Female*	0.576	9.39
Metropolitan*	0.280	2.60
Rural*	−0.023	−0.33
Primary*	0.112	1.69
Secondary*	0.441	5.13
Tertiary*	−0.113	−0.30
Migrated*	−0.276	−3.12
Married*	−0.313	−3.86
Head primary*	−0.134	−1.92
Head secondary*	−0.090	−0.88
Head tertiary*	−0.017	−0.06
Catholic*	−0.204	−2.41
Voodoo*	−0.372	−1.91
Other religions*	−0.310	−3.18
Constant	5.124	3.09

Note: No. observations: 2859. * is a discrete dummy variable; t is the test of the underlying coefficient being equal to 0. Household heads excluded. Variables omitted: urban, no education, head no education, Baptist.
Source: Authors' calculations based on HLCS 2001.

plausible indicators are available, including the prevalence of reciprocal labor arrangements in rural areas, migrant household relations, perceptions of violence, trust in institutions, and crime and homicide rates. These indicators suggest that robust social cohesion on the community level has been crucial in preventing Haiti's institutional-political crisis from deteriorating into widespread social collapse or civil war. For most of the rural population, fear is not a major concern. However, the demographic and economic trends described above are undermining some of the foundations of Haiti's traditional social cohesion, and will place heavy responsibilities on the state for maintaining social order in the future.

Rural Haitians have a history of undertaking certain types of work that require a concentrated effort in different kids of reciprocal, collective labor groups, such as the *coumbite*, the *eskwad*, and the *societé de travail*. These groups are important social institutions in rural

---

48. Family size and family size squared were statistically insignificantly different from zero.

49. The result may also stem from the fact that Baptists are more likely to stay in school; Baptists who drop out are a group with lower mean characteristics than their peer group of dropouts—that is, unobserved heterogeneity (Justesen 2004; Heckman and Singer 1984).

Haiti, both for mobilizing labor and as social, festive events.[50] Some observers have predicted the demise of these institutions in an ever more impoverished peasant economy, but 2001 data show that as many as 38 percent of cultivators used either *coumbites* or *eskwads*, in addition to household members, in their most recent harvest. This figure may be lower than would have been the case some decades ago, but it shows the continued vitality of these collective groups in rural communities. In comparison, only 16 percent of the farmers had hired individual paid labor.[51]

As seen above, internal and external migration is widespread. The extent to which migrants maintain contact with their families is an indicator of the strength of the bonds between households—that is, between the migrants' new household and the one they left behind.[52] The possibility of intertemporal family contracts is also of great economic relevance, because of the potential of migration as a source of financial capital via remittances.

Surprisingly, given the limited outreach of basic services in Haiti and their reputedly poor performance, the large majority of Haitians interviewed expressed confidence in schools, health services, and the police (see Table G.1 in Appendix G). All of these are given an "approval rating" of more than 60 percent by the rural population, and somewhat less in the cities. The schools rank highest with a 95 percent approval, which is far higher than school enrollment rates. Rather than an evaluation of performance, the statistics are best viewed as an expression of people's expectations of the various institutions. Thus political institutions—including parliament, the popular organizations, and the political parties—received a very low approval rating in 2001. Again, approval is positively correlated with the distance from those institutions: in rural areas, approval of political institutions is nearly double that in the metropolitan area. Surprisingly, traditional religious institutions, voodoo, and *houngans* receive the lowest approval rating of any of the institutions surveyed.

A more direct indicator of trust and social cohesion is whether people feel safe or afraid in various social situations (see Table G.2 in Appendix G). Results show sharp urban-rural differences: people in rural areas feel far safer in their daily lives than urban residents. As many as 58 percent of residents in the metropolitan area feel unsafe "often or most of the time" in their own homes, a reflection of severe problems of insecurity in the capital. In rural and other urban areas, on the other hand, "only" 15 percent feel unsafe at home. While a significant minority in rural areas also express fear of visiting markets and other towns, the data demonstrate that fear is not a major and daily concern for three-quarters of the rural population. These findings were supported by qualitative interviews conducted in rural areas in the spring of 2005 (Lamaute, Damais, and Egset 2005), when rural residents across the country indicated that the violent political conflict in Port-au-Prince and some other cities did not affect their personal safety. The conflict, however, did restrict the transportation of goods and people between regions and between rural and urban markets, significantly obstructing rural producers' access to regional and central markets.

---

50. For example, see Lundahl (1983) for more on the sociological roles of these work groups.

51. Authors' calculations based on HLCS (2001).

52. In economic theory, migration tends to be viewed either as an individual choice (especially Todaro, 1969 and later) motivated by an individual's economic incentives, or as a household diversification strategy regulated by an intertemporal family contract.

Domestic violence against women and children is the most prevalent form of violence in Haiti. According to the DHS (2001), 35 percent of women over 15 years old have been victims of physical violence, with a higher prevalence in provincial areas (41 percent) than in the metropolitan area (34 percent). Women and girls have also become targets of political and criminal violence. According to the UN Rapporteur (2000) on "Violence Against Women in Haiti," the phenomenon of *zenglendos*, or thugs, breaking into houses at any time, raping and beating women, started during the Cedras military regime as a form of political pressure but has now become a common practice of criminal gangs, terrorizing the entire population.

With regard to homicide rates, estimates based on HLCS 2001 suggest that Haiti has 33.7 homicides per 100,000 citizens,[53] which is somewhat higher than the regional average for the Latin American and Caribbean region (22.9 per 100,000), and about three times higher than the estimated global average of 10.7 homicides per 100,000 people. It is lower than rates in sub-Saharan Africa, where there is an average of 40 homicides per 100,000 people (Buvinic and Morrison, undated). Because the regional figures are from 1990 and homicide rates have probably increased since then in Latin America, it may be assumed that Haiti's homicide rates in an average year are on a par with the regional rate.

Whereas domestic violence reduces human security broadly throughout Haiti, criminal and political violence is largely concentrated in the metropolitan area and other urban hotspots, such as Cap Haitien and Gonaïve. The most recent wave of violence in Port-au-Prince spiked as of September 30, 2005, triggered by riots during the commemoration of the 1991 coup. According to the Incidents Database of the United Nations Stabilization Mission in Haiti (MINUSTAH), the total number of violent deaths in Haiti between June 2004 and May 2005 was 424 (see Figure 2.11). Of these, 323 deaths were in Port-au-Prince. Since the city has an estimated population of about 1.97 million (2003), this figure represents an annualized death rate of about 23 per 100,000 people, which is lower than Haiti's "normal" violent death rate. The number of violent deaths in Port-au-Prince has varied significantly from month to month, peaking in October 2004, December 2004, and April 2005, as shown in Figure 2.12. These fluctuations reflect the variations in (reported) violent death rates according to the shifting intensity of the conflict between gangs and the police/MINUSTAH.[54] Additionally, police sources report that 1,900 people were kidnapped between March and December 2005. The Chief of Police confirmed on January 9, 2006, that kidnapping rates in Haiti had risen to 20–24 a day.[55]

---

53. This estimate is based on the weighted number of violent deaths reported by all households (2,734), divided by the total population estimate. The unweighted number of violent deaths is nine.

54. MINUSTAH figures are thought to provide the most accurate reporting of violent deaths in the metropolitan area for the period in question. They include all reports of casualties from conflict, murders, bodies found in the streets, and other deaths reported to the police or to various branches of the UN. Nonetheless, they are likely to underreport deaths in which the police and MINUSTAH have not been involved, especially in those areas to which MINUSTAH or the police do not have access, notably the slum areas of Cité Soleil, Carrefour Feuille, and others. Other organizations have put the number of violent deaths in Port-au-Prince significantly higher, with up to 600 deaths between September 30, 2004, and May 2005 (International Crisis Group, "Spoiling Security in Haiti," *Latin America/Caribbean Report* N°13, May 31, 2005).

55. Control Risk Haiti Task Force, January 16, 2006.

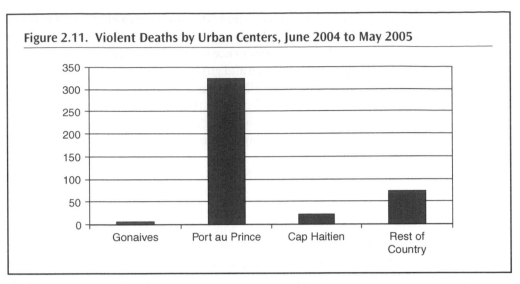

Figure 2.11. Violent Deaths by Urban Centers, June 2004 to May 2005

Source: MINUSTAH Incidence Database.

According to MINUSTAH, organized gangs concentrated in Bel Air and Cité Soleil are the most active criminal groups in Port-au-Prince and are considered responsible for the violence that has swept the capital, especially since September 2004. Figure 2.13 shows high-risk areas in the city according to MINUSTAH, as of April 2005. The neighborhoods of Martissant, Gran Ravine, Carrefour, Cité Soleil, and Bel Air all suffer from gang violence. MINUSTAH, however, reports that levels of violence are highest in Cité Soleil and Bel Air. From April to May 2005, kidnappings and other crimes increasingly spread from these areas to nearby areas, affecting industrial activities that are concentrated around the airport

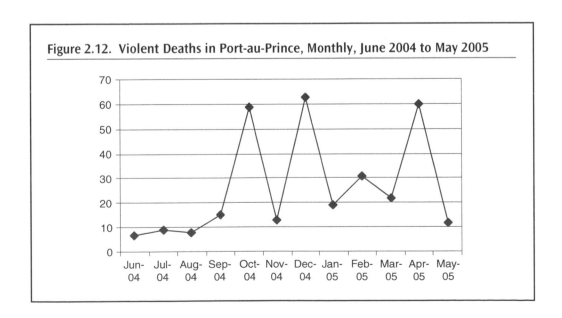

Figure 2.12. Violent Deaths in Port-au-Prince, Monthly, June 2004 to May 2005

Figure 2.13. High Crime Threat Areas in Port-au-Prince

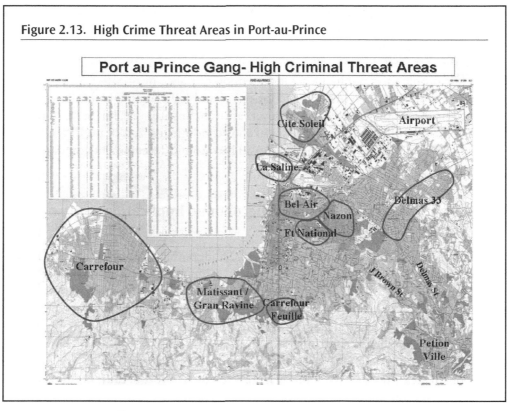

Source: MINUSTAH, April 2005.

and harbors near Cité Soleil. According to MINUSTAH sources,[56] gangs in Cité Soleil have sought to profit from these economic activities (by charging "protection" fees from business owners) and to disrupt economic activities, including commercial air traffic.

Gang violence is facilitated by the easy access to arms in Haiti, as documented by a Small Arms Survey completed in 2005 (Muggah 2005). At the time of this study, the number of available small arms was put at about 200,000, most of which are in the hands of civilians from all socioeconomic classes. Previous disarmament efforts have been largely unsuccessful and the national regulatory framework for arms control remains outdated and ineffective.

The drugs trade has also contributed to the escalation of crime and violence in Haiti. Haiti is not a significant producer of narcotics but it has become a major transshipment point for drug smuggling into the United States, a development facilitated by the weakness of law enforcement and border controls. The U.S. Drug Enforcement Administration has estimated that 15 percent of the cocaine entering the United States transits through either Haiti or the Dominican Republic, and has identified three main smuggling routes: via airdrops

---

56. Interview with MINUSTAH security officer, June 2005.

at sea, commercial shipping, and small coastal or shipping vessels.[57] As in other countries affected by the illicit drugs trade, competition for the control of the transshipment routes has led to an escalation of violent turf wars. According to MINUSTAH, drugs are mainly shipped through ports in the north and south of the country, and the individuals involved keep a low profile so as not to attract the attention of police or of MINUSTAH. Drugs-related corruption has also undermined the police and judiciary in Haiti. That matter is discussed further in the next section on governance and institutions, but more research is needed to foster understanding of the social and economic impacts of the drugs trade in Haiti and its implication for the state reform and economic development agendas.

Conclusion: Demographic and Socioeconomic Implications for Violence and Conflict Risk

This chapter has considered some of the main demographic and socioeconomic factors that contribute to Haiti's conflict-poverty trap. A high population growth rate, combined with rapid urbanization, is increasing the concentration of people in Haiti's cities, and in the metropolitan area in particular. This area now scores high on known demographic risk factors for violent conflict, including a very young population profile, a high population turnover due to high in- and out-migration, and a high rate of dissolved families. Overall population growth is slowly falling because of declining fertility rates, but migration to the metropolitan area is unlikely to diminish in the foreseeable future because of strong underlying socioeconomic incentives. New migrants are attracted to the metropolitan area every year by higher levels of infrastructure and services, greater access to formal and skilled jobs, and lower poverty levels than in all other parts of the country. In total, an estimated 115,000 job-seekers enter the metropolitan labor market every year, a labor market that offers very few opportunities and features a high unemployment rate. The capital's labor market has fewer total wage jobs than the number of new entrants every two years, and fewer skilled jobs than *one* year of new entrants. Unemployment is widespread as growing numbers of educated youth search for "good jobs" that are unlikely to materialize in the capital's small formal and skilled sectors, which have been shrunk by years of economic decline.

Against this backdrop, the pool of potential recruits for crime and violence thus continues to grow, while the opportunity costs of participating in illegal activities or political violence remain relatively low. As the population shifts from rural to urban areas, the robust social cohesion that has characterized the countryside becomes less effective in mitigating social dislocation. This places a heavy burden on state institutions to provide basic services that alleviate demographic and socioeconomic pressures, and to mitigate the negative outcomes of crime and conflict. As discussed in the next section, however, the state's institutional capacity to provide basic services and establish security and the rule of law will require significant strengthening if Haiti is to break out of its conflict-poverty trap.

---

57. Statement by Michael S. Vigil, Special Agent in Charge, Field Division, Drug Enforcement Administration, U.S. Department of Justice to the U.S. Congressional Subcommittee on Criminal Justice, Drug Policy and Human Resources, April 12, 2000, http://www.usdoj.gov/dea/pubs/cngrtest/ct041200.htm.

CHAPTER 3

Governance and Institutions

By Willy Egset and Stephanie Kuttner

Institutions matter for social and economic development,[58] and are crucial for state building and conflict prevention. Institutions have the potential to mitigate the risk factors of violence and conflict that emanate from the socioeconomic and demographic context, as indicated in the analytical model applied in this report. The Haitian state, however, has only a limited capacity to provide services that are essential to law and order, economic growth, poverty reduction and redistribution. It is argued that progress in breaking out of the conflict-poverty trap demands attention to the restoration of core state functions. This chapter provides some brief historical background to shed light on how the nature of Haiti's state institutions originated, and then examines the status of some of these core state functions—nationwide administrative control, basic services, and police and the judiciary. All of these functions are crucial to state-building, and to creating an enabling environment for economic development and poverty reduction.

Functions of the State

In classic state theory, the state originates in and is justified by citizens, who confer sovereignty on a central authority in exchange for security, broadly defined.[59] Security is fundamental in modern understandings and expectations of the state, but the concept of security

---

58. This now famous and widely accepted observation comes from North (1994).

59. State failure stems from the state's inability to credibly enforce security of life and transactions over a sustained period; the intensity and nature of violence is only a symptom of this underlying problem, not its definition. See Rotberg (2003). That study does not give a single definition of state failure but argues that it is not defined by the intensity of violence, but rather by the multiple challenges to state authority arising from the failure to hold the legitimate monopoly on force.

has widened.[60] As the concept of human security is used increasingly, security is considered by many to derive not only from an absence of physical violence, but also of hunger, disease, natural disasters, and economic deprivation, as well as access to political rights.[61] Most recent policy documents on state responsibilities include some broader human security concerns. For example, the 1997 World Development Report on the state described investments in basic social services as a fundamental state task without which "development is impossible."[62] Different sources suggest different core tasks,[63] but most concur in the primacy of the state's responsibility to provide pure public goods, chiefly security and the rule of law.

The pure public goods[64] in the upper left quadrant of Table 3.1[65] are the essentials of state-building and development, the sine qua non to which other functions and objectives may be added as the state's resources and capabilities grow. When these tasks are fulfilled, the state may extend the *scope* of its activities to a range of equity-improving interventions, or expand the *strength* of its activities within a limited range of activities, or both. It is very

---

60. Cf. also Collier et al. (2003): "In such conditions [of low, declining, and badly distributed incomes] the state is also likely to be weak, non-democratic, and incompetent, offering little impediment to the escalation of rebel violence, and maybe even provoking it."

61. UN Human Security Commission (2003).

62. The WDR 1997 on *The State in a Changing World* (World Bank 1997) identified five "fundamental tasks that lie at the core of every government's mission, without which sustainable, shared, poverty reducing development is impossible": (a) establishing a foundation of law; (b) maintaining a nondistortionary policy environment, including macroeconomic stability; (c) investing in basic social services and infrastructure; (d) protecting the vulnerable; and (e) protecting the environment. Note, however, that the state's task is to ensure and facilitate the provision of such basic services, not necessarily to be the provider itself.

63. For example, North (1991) identifies the following basic institutions as necessary for a modern economy to emerge: (a) secure property rights; (b) a polity and judicial system; (c) flexible laws that allow a range of organizational structures; and (d) the creation of complex governance structure to limit the problems of agency in hierarchical organizations. In a recent concept paper outlining "an approach to state building," Ashraf Ghani suggests 10 state functions that should be priorities for state building: (i) legitimate monopoly on the means of violence; (ii) administrative control; (iii) management of public finances; (iv) investment in human capital; (v) delineation of citizenship rights and duties; (vi) provision of infrastructure services; (vii) formation of the market; (viii) management of the state's assets; (ix) international relations; and (x) rule of law (Ashraf, Lockhard, and Carnahan 2005).

64. Public goods are goods that would not be provided in a free-market system, because firms would not be able to charge for them adequately. This situation arises because public goods have two particular characteristics. They are: (a) non-excludable—once the goods are provided, it is not possible to exclude people from using them even if those people have not paid. This allows "free-riders' to consume the good without paying; and (b) non-rival—consumption of the goods by one person does not diminish the amount available for the next person. In defining the state's core tasks, the literature is often ambiguous on basic services that are not pure public goods (typically, basic health and education services), and therefore are at least partly supplied by the market. Because of the high external collective benefits of these services, as well as equity and access concerns, it is reasonable to include these among the state's core functions (Mills et al. 2001). These "merit goods" are goods that could be provided in a free-market system but would almost certainly be underprovided, because market only takes account of the private costs and benefits. It does not take account of the external benefits that may arise for society if everyone were to enjoy the good in question—education, for example. If the private sector will not provide these goods in a sufficient quantity, then the population's needs will only be met if the government provides incentives for firms to produce more (perhaps by subsidizing the good or service), or if the government provides them itself. (From Institute for Fiscal Studies (IFS) Virtual Economy: http://www.bized.ac.uk/virtual/economy/policy/tools/government/gexpth2.htm.

65. This framework builds on World Bank (1997) and modifications suggested by Fukuyama (2004).

Table 3.1. Functions of the State

	Addressing market failure			Improving equity
Minimal functions	*PROVIDING PURE PUBLIC GOODS:* Defense, law and order Property rights Infrastructure* Macroeconomic management Public health			*Protecting the poor:* Antipoverty programs Disaster relief
Intermediate functions	*Addressing externalities:* Basic education Environmental protection	*Regulating monopoly:* Utility regulation Antitrust policy	*Overcoming imperfect information:* Insurance Financial regulation Consumer protection	*Providing social insurance:* Redistributive pensions Family allowances Unemployment insurance
Activist functions	*Coordinating private activity:* Fostering markets Cluster initiatives			*Redistribution:* Asset redistribution

Scope of state functions →

Strength of state institutions →

Source: World Bank 1997: Table 1.1.* Infrastructure is not included in the original table, but safe water and roads are discussed in the associated text, along with other pure public goods (World Bank 1997).

45

difficult for a state to move successfully in either direction until it has effectively established pure public goods.

Drawing on these perspectives of the state's core tasks, the following section assesses the Haitian state's capacity to deliver certain basic state functions: national administrative control (a precondition for planning and providing appropriate services); basic social services; and, most essentially, security and the rule of law.[66] The first two parts of the section are largely descriptive, to provide (a) a background for understanding the socioeconomic processes and outcomes discussed in the previous section and (b) a realistic baseline for future work and development assistance in these policy areas. The third section analyses the security and rule of law sectors in more detail, and reviews lessons learned from a decade of largely unsuccessful reform efforts.

Haiti's Fragile State

Haiti has never had a tradition of governance that seeks to provide services to the population or create an environment conducive to sustainable growth. Instead, a small economic elite has supported a "predatory state" that has made only negligible investments in human resources and basic infrastructure (World Bank 1998). It ranks among the bottom 5 percent of countries in the World Bank Institute's Aggregate Governance Indicators, which measure voice and accountability, political stability, government effectiveness, regulatory quality, rule of law, and control of corruption (Kaufmann, Kraay, and Mastruzzi 2005). With a long history of government neglect of basic public service provision, and the legacy of a paternalistic and repressive dictatorship that lasted for three decades between 1957 and 1986, the Haitian state today is largely absent from the lives of most citizens.[67]

To understand the state's capacity to drive development, its fundamental financial constraints must first be noted. Haiti's GDP is extremely low and has been declining since 1980. In 2005, central government revenues were only 9 percent of GDP,[68] compared to an average of 18 percent among other low-income countries and 32 percent in high-income countries. Only 1.8 percent of revenues derive from taxes on income, profits, or capital.[69] Central government expenditures have fluctuated sharply—between 9 and 16 percent of GDP in recent years—as a result of volatility in external assistance (IMF 2005). Thus a weak domestic revenue base, unstable external flows, and poor expenditure targeting have left spending on education, health, and infrastructure in Haiti below the average of low-income countries.

---

66. This analysis will not address macroeconomic management or and public economic governance in general, since those matters are the focus of a separate, forthcoming World Bank study (Haiti Country Economic Memorandum, forthcoming).

67. The political economy of the origin of government passivity, which is related to the transition to small-scale peasant agriculture in the first decades of the nineteenth century, is analyzed at length in Lundahl (1979, 1983).

68. See Center on International Cooperation and Political Economy Research Institute (2005): Public Finance and Post-Conflict Statebuilding. Meeting of Case Study Authors and Advisory Committee, Meeting Summary.

69. As a result of a series of "complete exemptions . . . [and] generous deductions" (IMF 2005) on both personal and corporate taxes.

A Legacy of Public Sector Corruption

Haiti has a long history of public office being used to secure private gain. Under the Duvalier regimes, the concentration of authority in the unsalaried position of the *chef de section* paved the way for widespread corruption and abuse of power (Lahav 1975). In July 2005, the government's Central Unit on Economic and Financial Investigations (UCREF) reported that several million dollars of public funds had been diverted via a private shell company to Lavalas-linked organizations.[70] Most recently, in response to reports of corruption and mismanagement by interim government officials and the judiciary, the interim prime minister announced an investigation into the finances of all public agencies and the courts.[71]

Haiti ranked 155 among the 158 countries surveyed in Transparency International's 2005 Corruption Perception Index. Transparency International's national chapter surveyed 315 heads of household in Port-au-Prince and the surrounding communities, as well as 40 private businesses, and found that public sector corruption was perceived to be widespread.[72] With little opportunity in the private sector and a stagnant economy, individuals have few avenues for advancement outside the public sector.

There have been allegations of several forms of corruption and administrative malfeasance in Haiti. These include corruption in the institutions responsible for upholding the rule of law—the police and the judiciary (as discussed below); embezzlement of public funds by political and private organizations; payments to government-associated individuals for goods that were not provided and services that were not rendered; abuse of discretionary accounts by government officials; and evasion of the licensing fees and import tariffs collected by public enterprises.[73]

In 2004, the Interim Government of Haiti created an anti-corruption unit, a financial investigation unit, and a commission to examine Haitian government transactions between 2001 and February 2004. With the support of the World Bank Institute's Governance and Anti-Corruption Initiative, a survey of "governance and perceptions of corruption in Haiti" has recently been undertaken by the finance ministry's anti-corruption unit; the results are expected later this year.

Difficult Donor Partnerships

Following an international embargo during the military regime (1992–94), international assistance was revived with the return of President Aristide and constitutional order to Haiti, and continued during the presidency of René Préval (1995–2000). The electoral crisis of 2000, however, as well as concerns about growing political interference and corruption,

70. *Miami Herald,* "Aristide diverted millions," August 4, 2005.
71. *Miami Herald,* "Haiti's interim leader orders corruption probe," April 12, 2006.
72. La Fondation heritage pour Haiti, "The State of Corruption in Haiti" (2003).
73. The government-established Commission of Administrative Inquiries (CEA), headed by Paul Denis (who later became a presidential candidate of the Struggling People's Organization, OPL), published an interim report on corruption in government administration in July 2005. Portions of the CEA's report have been posted on a website: http://haitianmofo.blogspot.com/2005/07/emperor-has-no-clothes.html.

led donors to withdraw institutional support abruptly and to channel most of their assistance through the private sector and civil society.

While political crises have prompted the withdrawal of donor support to the public sector, the very weakness of institutional capacities in Haiti has been identified as the main factor undermining the effectiveness of development assistance. In a 2002 evaluation of the unsatisfactory impact of its assistance to Haiti, the World Bank concluded that "the Bank and other donors erred in offering traditional assistance programs without identifying the fundamental governance and political barriers to development, and by overwhelming [Haiti's] fragile absorptive capacity" (World Bank 2002). In a 2004 review of a "Decade of Difficult Partnership", the Canadian International Development Agency, Haiti's second largest bilateral donor, suggested moving away from reactive, political triggers for aid-allocation and towards an engagement based on analysis of structural challenges and opportunities, in partnership with government, donors, and civil society (CIDA 2004).

In 2004, donors sought to strengthen coordination and move towards harmonization of international assistance through joint preparation of the Interim Cooperation Framework (ICF) with the Transitional Government of Haiti. The ICF established sectoral priorities for development assistance, budget requirements, and targets and results indicators over the 2004–2006 period. During this process, donors recognized that a past "policy of massive investment, followed by sudden withdrawal, is counter-productive and that it is important to maintain the public sector's organizational and institutional capacity."[74] They also acknowledged that a lack of coordination, consistency, and strategic vision in their interventions, combined with a tendency to set up parallel project implementation structures, had weakened the state without giving it the means to coordinate external aid and improve national absorptive and execution capacities.

An Unfinished Decentralization

The small size of the government is reflected in the limited national outreach of the public administration. Historically, the basic administrative unit for both civilian and military administration was the *section rurale* or rural section, governed by a *chef de section* or section chief under military tutelage. Local civic councils (*Conseil d'administration de la section rurale*-CASER) were constitutionally mandated but never established before 1987. In the Duvalier period (1957–86), the *chef de section* was usually a local resident with connections to central political power, who was directly appointed by the president. The *chef* held all local powers, including the general administration of the *section rurale*, judicial responsibilities (mediation of local disputes, adjudication of civil and criminal cases), and police functions (maintenance of public order, criminal investigations).

Under Duvalier, Councils for Community Action, largely controlled by militias (*Volontaires de la Sécurité Nationale*, VSN), also played a key role in the political control exercised in rural areas by mobilizing labor for public works. They also prevented peasant organizations from forming and infiltrated the existing groups. The vast majority of the rural population was thus excluded and had little voice in local or central decision-making.

---

74. The Republic of Haiti, Interim Cooperation Framework, Summary Report, July 2004, p. 5.

Instead, they were subject to multiple fiscal burdens such as export taxes on coffee, market taxes, as well as import and sales taxes on primary necessities (Girault 1980).

Against the backdrop of the Duvalier regime's concentration and abuse of power, and mainly to circumscribe presidential authority, the 1987 democratic constitution served the objectives of political decentralization and established checks and balances between local and central government, as well as among government branches. The constitution prescribed a comprehensive structure of local and regional governance, the Territorial Collectivities or *Collectivités Territoriales* (CT). The constitution gives the CTs wide but unclear responsibilities, including public order, the selection of judges, the formation of the Permanent Electoral Council, local education, literacy, tax systems, and other forms of public administration. Central authorities are represented in the provinces through a system of government delegates in each of Haiti's 10 (since 2005) regions or departments, and vice delegates in each of the approximately 40 localities or *arrondissements*. This formal structure is described in Table F.3 in Appendix F.

The CTs are organized under a dual structure of deliberative and executive branches on most administrative levels, including the smallest administrative unit of the *section communale* or communal section, the *commune* or commune, and the *département* or department. The Administrative Council of the Section Communale (CASEC) has responsibility for carrying out the decisions of the Assembly of the Section Communale (ASEC). Its role is that of public administration at the local level, especially maintaining infrastructure and participating in local development activities. At the national level, the Interdepartmental Council (CID) represents the regions in department-wide issues, and the CID in turn is entitled to representation in relevant debates at the central government level. The system is meant to ensure a line of accountability from lower to higher levels: the Municipal Council reports to the Municipal Assembly, which reports to the Departmental Council, which reports to the Departmental Assembly, which finally is accountable to the Interdepartmental Council.

The complexity of the system of *Collectivités Territoriales* has made it difficult to implement in practice. Among its many institutions, only the CASEC and *commune* have been operational, at least for certain periods since 1987. Even during periods of national political breakdown these local institutions have shown a capacity to remain operational to some degree. Although locally relevant and active, they have been weakened by a lack of financial and other resources and by the unclear nature of their responsibilities. No unified law defines the exact mandates of the various CT levels and bodies. Because CT structures have never been established at the regional and national levels, the system has not performed its anticipated role as a means of transmission between local representation and central government. The CT structure has thus become marginalized and ineffectual, and has had little effect on policy-making to date.

Since 2004 the CTs have been in a state of suspended animation. The mandate of local officials (CASECs) elected in 2000 ended in 2004; some continued in office, and others were reappointed by the transitional government, as were mayors. Local elections were initially scheduled to take place in 2005 but they were postponed indefinitely while the transitional government and the international community focused on the presidential and legislative elections. The uncertainty of this situation leaves the way open for local strongmen to reassert their power, a process that sometimes includes the return of former section chiefs (Lamaute, Damais, and Egset 2005). In place of an overly complex formal structure, in practice there is an institutional void. This perpetuates the absence of channels for political expression on the part of the rural population in particular, and prevents the flow of information between local communities and central authorities (and international donors) that could enhance the effectiveness of national development policies.

Infrastructure and Basic Services

The weakness of nationwide administrative and political governance structures is matched by the very limited provision of basic infrastructure services (roads, potable water, electricity, telephone lines) outside the metropolitan area (see Chapter 2). Public spending on the social sectors is similarly low. Public domestic financing of education in 2006 is projected to be just 1.7 percent of GDP, the lowest in the LAC region, where the average is 5 percent. If all donor financing is included in the calculation, public financing for education increases to 2.1 percent of GDP. Public domestic financing of the health sector in 2006 only reached 1.26 billion gourdes. On the demand side, low and fluctuating income often leads to a declining demand because of the limited capacity to pay for services. Fees for even basic services account for a significant proportion of family income.

Very little public social and productive assistance is provided in Haiti. Social protection, for example, is only accessible in the form of a pension for public sector workers. There is no public safety net and only a handful of private or NGO-run programs. The main source of social benefits is the ministry of social affairs and employment (MAST). Its assistance covers only formal sector workers, who represent just 3 percent of all workers in Haiti. Total public spending by MAST was less than US$7 million in 2004, or less than 1.7 percent of the national budget. This declined to less than US$5 million in the 2005 budget. Sixty percent of this spending was for MAST staff, more than three-quarters of whom are administrative and service employees (as opposed to technical or professional-level personnel). The few other social service providers have very limited budgets and thus provide only minimal coverage. The Social and Economic Assistance Fund (FAES) has functioned relatively well as a provider of basic infrastructure but it has suffered a decline in budget and personnel. The net results of limited domestic funding, inefficient use of scarce public funds (with budgets often swollen by personnel expenses), and limits on absorptive capacity for external funding are major gaps in social protection.

Despite this minimal state intervention, which has been compounded by continued economic decline since 1980, many social indicators have steadily improved in recent decades (see Chapter 2), although they remain significantly below regional averages. A partial explanation for this paradox is that basic education and health services are not pure public-supplied goods but are partly market-supplied. In addition, subsidized and non-profit NGOs are exceptionally important service providers in the health and education sectors.

The Role of the Non-State Sector in the Provision of Basic Services

Many developing countries, especially fragile states, depend significantly on non-state providers (NSPs) for the provision of basic services to parts of the population, typically the poorest.[75] In such contexts, NSPs are crucial in giving people access to services. They have also been found to be more responsive to markets and to offer better quality and more competitive, cost-effective services than the state (Mills and others 2002). NSPs may also be less susceptible than the public sector to political change and conflict.

NSPs in health and education tend to operate at both ends of the quality spectrum, offering either an elite service for the wealthy, or informal but accessible (though often poor quality) services for those who are poor and lack access to formal and subsidized state services. Operators may be communities, NGOs, faith-based organizations, private companies, small-scale informal providers, and individual practitioners (Moran and Batley 2004). The non-state sector in Haiti is very diverse; a breakdown of six main categories of NSPs is given in Table F.2 of Appendix F. This heterogeneity makes regulation, coordination, and quality assurance challenging. Moreover, service provision by the non-state sector also poses questions about the equity and quality of service provision. This is problematic for individual consumers and for the collective welfare of the country as a whole. Additionally, donor-assisted NSPs may create parallel structures and help debilitate already weak government structures (Ghani and others 2005). Such concerns suggest that the state has an important role in service provision at some level. In fragile states with limited resources and capacity, governments may be better placed to facilitate and coordinate than to engage in direct provision.

As Chapter 2 shows, education is the single most important determinant of an individual's potential to escape poverty in Haiti. The non-state sector has been crucial in making this progress despite formidable economic and political constraints. The Haitian state's role in primary education is uniquely low from a global perspective. Of the world's 20 poorest countries, Haiti is the only one in which more than 50 percent of children are enrolled in non-state schools.[76] The country has a total of 14,424 private schools and 1,240 public schools. Non-state schools therefore comprise 92 percent of all schools, the vast majority of which do not receive public subsidies. Some 82 percent of all primary and secondary school students attend private, fee-based schools (MENJS 2003). Public schools are mainly in urban areas.

State health service provision is similarly limited. The shortage of trained staff, clinics, funds, and essential drugs and equipment hamper the provision of state health services. The Inter-American Development Bank (IDB) estimates that only about 30 percent of health facilities in Haiti are public, and most of them are located in urban areas. Razafimandimby (2006) reports that 75 percent of doctors and 67 percent of nurses work in the West region and there are virtually no doctors outside the capital in public health centers. Through cooperation with Cuba established in the 1990s to increase access to health care in remote areas, several hundred Cuban health professionals have been deployed throughout Haiti.[77] Yet health indicators for rural areas remain poor. Chronic malnutrition (stunting),

---

75. In sub-Saharan Africa, NGO hospitals provide 43 percent of medical work in Tanzania; 40 percent in Malawi, and 34 percent in Ghana. In Asia, the figures are 26 percent for Taiwan, 15 percent for India, and 12 percent for Indonesia (Medicus Mundi International, n.d.).

76. The exception is Zimbabwe, where even higher levels of children are enrolled in private primary education but where private schools receive government subsidies.

77. UN Press Conference on Humanitarian Aid, New York, March 23, 2004, http://www.un.org/News/briefings/docs/2004/CanadaPressCfc.doc.htm

for example, is estimated at 22 percent among children below 5 years of age, and only 22 percent of children receive all standard vaccines, although about 70 percent receive some key vaccines such as that for tuberculosis (DHS 2001).

NGO health service provision has developed mainly outside the capital, although the slums of Port-au-Prince are also areas of attention in this respect. NGOs provide an estimated 70 percent of health services in rural areas and focus in particular on primary health care, including reproductive health, drug counseling, infant care, and HIV/AIDS screening. There are a number of hospitals run by private foundations but the state retains the main responsibility for secondary and tertiary care, as well as for overall oversight and referral (coordinating non-state primary healthcare providers with state hospitals).

These statistics are borne out by two recent qualitative studies that examined the role of community service providers in rural communities and slum neighborhoods in Port-au-Prince (Lamaute and others 2005; Egset and Mattner 2005). In both areas, the studies found a diverse and sometimes surprisingly dense environment of service providers. Urban slums are marked by the strong presence of community organizations in areas such as sanitation, drinking water, healthcare, education, and even electricity provision. Public utilities are the main providers of water (CAMEP) and electricity (EDH) but that circumstance does not ensure equal access. For example, Cité Soleil, a stronghold of Lavalas supporters, had much better access to these services than the equally poor but less politicized Carrefour Feuille slum (Egset and Mattner 2005). Despite the presence of many providers, access to services is patchy, unstable, and unequal, reflecting political considerations in initial provision, poor maintenance capacity, a low level of coordination, and the violence and crime that affect service supply and demand.

In Haiti's rural areas, conventionally considered a "*vide institutionel*" or institutional void, many and diverse service providers exist, including community-based groups, national and international NGOs, and some public institutions. In the surveyed communities, basic and health services were available from a large number of providers at relatively low cost, but the very poorest cannot afford them. In many communities, users reported making great efforts to pay for private schools rather than rely on the public schools that, when available, were the only recourse for the poorest. Agricultural inputs, technical assistance, and credit are also provided by many actors, though with large regional variations. There were several agricultural support projects in surveyed communities with high agricultural potential (such as Laborde and Roche Plate), but support was practically nonexistent in areas with low potential in the North and Northwest regions. In those areas, to the dismay of many respondents, development projects focus solely on social safety nets. Users of farm assistance services frequently complained about the instability and costs of such services. These variations add risks to production decisions and thereby discourage greater commercialization (Lamaute and others 2005).

Basic Services: Access, Quality, and Equity

Broadening access to services is perhaps the most significant contribution of the non-state sector in Haiti. In the absence of public provision of basic services, private providers have made the difference between no education and some kind of schooling for large parts of the population. The same is true of health and other services. In rural areas especially, the non-state sector has provided a crucial safety net by offering access to services to a population mostly unserved by the state. Nonetheless, the costs of these essential services still hamper the access of large groups and the overall quality of the services is deficient.

Among both private and public providers, the general quality of health and education services varies substantially. Private-sector services have replaced public investment rather than complemented it, and their rapid and unchecked growth has significantly under-mined efficiency and equity (Salmi 1998). According to some studies, 60 percent of teach-ers in non-public schools are unqualified and many informal and disreputable educational establishments operate without licenses in inadequate environments. A snapshot of the education sector reveals an elite category of private schools (usually religious and urban-based) that have established themselves at the top of the pile[78] and are affordable only to the wealthiest. These are followed by a large group of public schools that occupy the middle of the range, and then by the vast majority of private schools at the bottom (Salmi 1998).

More positively, the NGO sector has shown itself to be resistant to political turmoil and can draw on a pool of highly motivated leaders who are committed to maintaining services during crises. Staff motivation is judged to be relatively high within the non-state sector, and some performance-based compensation systems have been introduced suc-cessfully.[79] Parent-teacher associations (PTAs) appear to be more successful and influential in the non-state sector than in the public sector because of greater parental involvement. PTAs in the non-state sector have fostered community participation, encouraged trans-parency, and tackled issues such as insecurity. As a result, they have made school manage-ment more democratic.

Improving the education system and broadening access to education—especially that of the poor—will require a series of actions and reforms that seek to: (i) increase the public resources allocated to education; (ii) strengthening the capacity and capability of the state to better fulfill its planning, coordination and normative responsibilities; and (iii) adopting proactive reforms to tackle demand-side constraints. The ultimate goal should be no less than universal primary education by 2015, as promoted by the Education For All Fast Track Initiative (EFA-FTI) program, which is supported by a wide range of national and international agencies.[80]

In the health sector, a plethora of unqualified healers and voodoo remedies prompt concern, although traditional healers and midwives make valuable contributions. Poor Haitians generally seek various cures depending on their ailment, but overall their ability to choose is limited by geographical and financial constraints on both demand and supply. As with school-selection, households have limited capacity to judge the quality of care because of the population's low level of education (Mills and others 2001). Often they seek

---

78. This is true, for example, of the non-state schools that belong to one of the major platforms (FONHEP, CONFEPIH) or networks (such as those supported within the USAID network); these receive regular visits from inspectors, as well as training and support. Inspection visits are an important accountability mech-anism between the schools and the associations themselves, which have a vested interest (reputation) in ensuring that standards are maintained.

79. The USAID experience in Haiti shows that NGOs providing services can respond to incentives and financing systems that are based on performance-based payment, which clearly improved their efficiency, effectiveness, and accountability (Eichler and Pollock 2001).

80. The EFA-FTI was created in 2002 to accelerate progress towards the 2015 Millennium Development Goal of universal primary education. See http://www1.worldbank.org/education/efafti/overview.asp.

health treatment from low-cost providers whose remedies fall far short of modern medical standards. This is particularly problematic for people living with HIV/AIDS.

Prices, like quality, vary significantly among NSPs. High-quality services and advanced treatment (hospitalization) are prohibitively expensive and unavailable in rural areas, but fees in the general NGO health sector may be donor-subsidized and thus sometimes lower than in the state sector.[81] Household income, however, remains the main constraint on access to health and education services in the non-state sector (Razafimandimby 2006). School fees are estimated to account for between 15 and 25 percent of rural households' expenditures, evidencing the priority given to education in Haiti, even among poor families. Nonetheless, as discussed in Chapter 2, the cost barrier is reflected in sharp differences in schooling across economic strata: net primary school enrolment is 54 percent in the lowest quintile, compared to 75 percent in the highest.[82] In the health sector, and despite some cross-subsidization schemes, user fees impede the poorest's access to essential medicines and treatment. Major health problems are therefore important causes of asset-depletion, since even the less poor might have to sell land, livestock or other assets to cover sudden costs so that they can save their own lives or that of their children. This process is a cause of downward mobility among vulnerable groups in rural areas (Lamaute, Damais, and Egset 2005).

Finally, the diverse and unregulated nature of basic service-provision can be exploited by political interests that use access as a means of bestowing patronage, garnering support, and gaining leverage. In Cité Soleil, for example, especially in the Grouillard and Bois-Neuf neighborhoods, water points have come under the control of armed groups that determine the distribution and sale of potable water and that appropriate the revenues raised. This development has been at the expense of the Potable Water System Management Committee (*Comité de Gestion du Système d'Eau Potable*) put in place by the CAMEP, which receives no share of the revenues. In Fort-Mercredi, a CAMEP project to provide drinking water has faced threats from some *baz* (gangs) to ensure that the water lines will run through their territory (Egset and Mattner 2005).

The Problem of State Regulation and Coordination

Little effort is made in the non-state sector to identify which areas are least served and to target services accordingly, although large donor programs have made some attempt to broaden coverage through the development of sectoral networks. Some information is available in the education sector about school distribution and underserved areas but this is not always taken into account by NGOs, which tend to concentrate their efforts in regions where they have other activities under way. The lack of coordination seems to be fueled by competition and lack of trust among some NSPs. Public sector service provision also suffers coordination problems that contribute to inequitable access and coverage. The

---

81. Estimates for the cost of a consultation in a state clinic varied between US$2 and US$6, excluding the cost of medicines or tests. In NGO clinics, both consultation costs and medicines are generally subsidized. Most providers have to charge fees for drugs and consultations, and such charges are beyond the reach of many people.

82. HLCS (2003).

coordination of state services is also hampered by inadequate management information systems, strategies that are not put into operation with any level of detail, and the lack of government leadership in playing a convening role.

Several efforts have been made to enhance coordination among service providers and the quality of oversight and standardization. On the most basic operational level, public-private health partnerships have consisted of the state reaching agreements with NSPs to provide child immunization programs and prenatal care to pregnant women within their local catchment areas. These programs have been important but not systematic. On a regulatory level, the state has tried to carve out a role for itself as a regulator of education through an accreditation system. Schools can circumvent this restriction, however, and fewer than a quarter of all non-state schools are accredited (nearly all of them in urban areas) because the incentives to register are insufficient (Razafimandimby 2006). On the national regulatory level, the ministries of health and education have developed national sectoral plans. These are generally deemed coherent and appropriate.[83] Additionally, several structures within the various ministries have attempted to provide a more enabling environment for systematic coordination. The most important of these structures is the National Partnership Office (*Office Nationale de Partenariat*, ONP), a still-incipient initiative established by the government in December 1999. The office is currently being relaunched as a focal point for NSP coordination and public-private partnership.[84] Among other things, the ONP will promote the establishment of the public-private partnership model EFACAP (*Ecole Fondamentale d'Application/Centre d'Appui Pedagogique*). This model seeks to create a network of (public or private) educational establishments affiliated with a publicly-funded center. The center's role is to establish standards and regulations for teacher training, participatory school management, and the restoration and improvement of facilities.

In the health sector, the District Health Center (*Unité Central de Santé*, UCS) is a more decentralized partnership model whose goal is likewise to establish a better partnership between the public and non-state sectors. In both sectors, however, an enabling environment for public-private partnerships has yet to be facilitated through legal frameworks, charters, and policy guidelines.

The main weakness of policy-making and coordination appears to be that sectoral strategies, plans, and organizational structures are of limited operational use. Both the health and education sectors seem to lack detailed plans of how to implement these strategies, and that include definitions of responsibilities, roles, and impact indicators. That circumstance seems to stem partly from the weak institutional capacity of both sectors at the central level, which causes further institutional weaknesses at the local level. There is inadequate analysis of information and basic data, a lack of action plans and priorities at the departmental and commune levels, an absence of job descriptions for school inspectors, a

---

83. The National Education Plan focuses on the same four key objectives that it has for some years: increasing access, improving quality, enhancing the efficiency of the system, and good governance. The national strategic health plan for 2005–2010 has been created and approved, but it lacks explicit operational guidelines for the implementation of the law.

84. USAID and the World Bank (LICUS) are currently working with the Haitian government to develop the state's capacity to design and implement this system.

shortage of coordination within the sector, and little support for reform-minded leaders. Because of the excessive centralization of public sector decision-making in the capital, local staff do not take responsibility for these problems. High staff turnover, moreover, results in limited institutional memory. While there is broad agreement on the need for coordination, therefore, and while plans have been made, constraints on operational implementation abound.

Security

The Haitian National Police

The Haitian National Police (HNP) was established with large-scale international support after the dissolution of the national army (*Forces Armées d'Haiti*, FAd'H) in 1995. Following an initial US-led multinational force, the first UN mission to Haiti (UNMIH) was deployed in October 1994. In addition to its traditional peacekeeping responsibilities, UNMIH was mandated to support the creation of a new national civilian police force.[85] A series of multidimensional UN peacekeeping missions followed, with mandates to support the recruitment, vetting and training of the HNP.[86] In addition to the UN support, a significant amount of bilateral assistance was provided for the HNP by the United States, Canada and France. The HNP was initially considered a success in internationally-assisted institution building, with a capable force of about 6,500 officers established between 1994 and 1997 (Kumar 2000). By the late 1990s, however, external financial aid to the government had been significantly reduced. The contested elections of 2000 then led to the suspension of most multilateral and bilateral programs, and support for the police was phased out by 2001.

The Office of the Inspector General (IG), established in June 1995, was created as the HNP's main internal mechanism for accountability on human rights abuses and adherence to domestic codes of conduct. It was endowed with powers to discipline police officers, terminate their employment or submit them for trial if they were accused of serious human rights violations or criminal conduct. In 1994 and 1995 there was some important early success in promoting accountability through the leadership of the first Inspector General who disciplined, suspended, and turned over for prosecution police officers allegedly guilty of misconduct and abuse (NCHR 1998). However, the IG's ability to effectively control police misconduct and abuse was undermined by the slowness of judicial reform (Stromsen and Trincellito 2003).

Institutional Capacity and Accountability

As an early sign of the political interference that would plague police reform in later years, several reformers were removed from leadership posts and some FAd'H officers who had

---

85. UN Security Council Resolution 867, September 22, 1993 (S/RES/867).
86. UNSMIH (1996–1997) and UNTMIH (1997). For more information, see http://www.un.org/Depts/dpko/missions/minustah/.

previously been vetted out were reinstated at the end of President Aristide's first term. Some of these decisions were reversed by President Préval (1995–2000), under whom progress was made in implementing institutional reforms (Stromsen and Trincellito 2003). In 1996 the new director general of the police identified politicization and corruption as the main threats to the professionalization of the HNP (NCHR 1998).

The HNP's effectiveness and credibility declined sharply from 2000 onwards. Police officers repeatedly acted in concert with gangs[87] in the final years of the Aristide period, a collusion that was promoted by the integration of members of armed gangs (*chimères*) into the police force itself (Tremblay 2004). Politicization and the weakness of accountability mechanisms within the HNP created a climate in which corruption and links to criminal networks and drug trafficking could be exploited (U.S. Department of State 2004). In 2000, UN Secretary General Kofi Annan referred to "worrying allegations of police involvement in robbery, extortion and abduction, as well as drug trafficking . . . and the involvement of popular organizations in protection rackets."[88] Several senior HNP officials, including a former director general, have since been convicted in the United States on drug trafficking-related charges.[89]

In 2001, President Aristide's announcement of an "Operation Zero Tolerance" crime-fighting initiative was widely considered a green light for police abuse and vigilante violence against real and alleged criminals (ICG 2004). By this time, international assistance to the HNP had effectively been withdrawn, as had other official development assistance to the government. The termination of government aid further increased the incentives for corruption within the police force as salaries became irregular, and the increasingly isolated government used the police to repress domestic enemies.[90] A series of reports by the Organization of American States (OAS 2001, 2003) documented the HNP's involvement in the December 17, 2001 attack on the national palace and in instigating the ensuing violence against the opposition, as well as the HNP's violent response to anti-government demonstrations. In July 2003, the director general of police resigned (the third in as many months), alleging that the president and his aides tried to run the police from the presidential palace (Carey 2003).

By February 2004, the HNP had practically collapsed in the face of an insurgent force of only a few hundred men with modest weapons. The current number of personnel is uncertain but official figures showed 4,500 officers in May 2005, assisted by 1,200 UN civilian police officers (UNPOL). Assuming that the force may have grown to 5,000 since then, the HNP remains one of the most numerically weak police forces in the world, with 63 officers per 100,000 citizens. This compares, for example, to 285 per 100,000 in the LAC region (Figure 3.1). Haiti now has more private security personnel than police officers.

---

87. According to a Human Rights Watch report (HRW 2001) on attacks on the opposition in 2001, "members of popular organizations supporting Fanmi Lavalas were responsible for violent street demonstrations and other mob actions that went largely unchallenged by the Haitian National Police . . . Police who were on the scene did not interfere, nor did they make any arrests."

88. Cited in Fatton (2002).

89. "Ex-Haiti Cop's Corruption Trial About to Begin," *Miami Herald,* September 20, 2005, and "Former Haitian Officer Cleared of Drug Charges," *Miami Herald,* October 8, 2005.

90. This point was made by James Dobbins, Rand Corporation, former U.S. envoy to Haiti, at the workshop on "Development, Security, and Statebuilding in Haiti," World Bank, November 15, 2005.

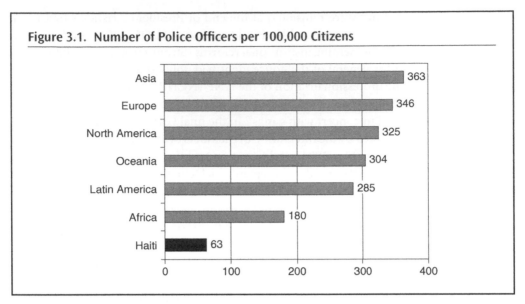

Figure 3.1. Number of Police Officers per 100,000 Citizens

Source: ICG 2005/UNODC 2005.

A director general leads the HNP and oversees a number of central and territorial directorates. Each of Haiti's nine departments has a director. Police chiefs (*commissaires*) head city police divisions. Sergeants (*inspecteurs*) head the subprecincts in smaller towns and the smallest police divisions in rural and urban sections. At the central level there are an separate administrative police (the main police corps) and judicial police (an investigative unit for the judiciary), an Inspector General, and a number of specialized units.[91] In practice, the HNP's organization and line of command nonetheless remain obscure, and its personnel and vehicles are commonly unidentified, circumstances that further diminish its effectiveness and the population's trust in it (ICG 2005).

After President Aristide's departure the remnants of the HNP were demoralized and in organizational disarray (ICG 2004). Several hundred officers were dismissed by the Transitional Government and a screening procedure for new recruits has since been established, but some 200 former soldiers were also integrated into the police in January 2005 without screening or training (ICG 2005). In addition to the old FAd'H officers in its high command, many HNP personnel have questionable backgrounds.[92] Human rights organizations continue to identify serious human rights violations by police officers, including direct involvement in the past year's wave of kidnappings (Human Rights Watch 2005; RNDDH 2005a). According to the director of the HNP, "about a quarter

91. The Palace and Presidential Guard, the Ministerial Security Corps, a crowd control unit (the Compagnie d'Intervention et Maintien d'Ordre, CIMO), and a special tactics team (the Groupe d'Intervention de la Police Nationale d'Haïti, GIPNH).

92. See, for example, interview with the Vice President of ICG, Mark Schneider, in the International Herald Tribune June 24, 2005.

of the force is involved in corruption, kidnappings or even arms trafficking"[93] (AP 10/11/05).

Police Reform

In April 2004, the UN Security Council established MINUSTAH with a mandate "to assist the Interim Government in monitoring, restructuring and reforming the Haitian National Police."[94] MINUSTAH, however, was not given executive authority over the HNP and it has been criticized by external observers and Haitian groups for failing to interpret its mandate more aggressively.[95] In June 2005, the Security Council called for greater coordination between MINUSTAH police and the HNP, as well as for the investigation of human rights violations by HNP officers, and reaffirmed MINUSTAH's authority to vet and certify new and existing HNP personnel.[96]

On March 15, 2005, the government's Superior Council of the National Police (*Conseil Supérieur de la Police Nationale*) adopted an HNP strategic reform plan for 2005–2008.[97] MINUSTAH's current program to assist HNP reform includes operational support through a co-location program (based on a memorandum of understanding with Haitian authorities); support for investigative capacity-building, particularly of the judicial police (with French bilateral assistance); recruitment and training of new officers (with Canadian bilateral assistance); support for the establishment of a vetting process for new recruits and serving officers (an initiative of the OAS and the United States); and establishing pilot projects in police stations for responding to female victims of violence and providing training on children's rights (with U.S. support) .

Numerous reports have indicated broad agreement on the lessons learned from international efforts to build an effective and capable national police force in Haiti in the 1990s (Stromsen and Trincellito 2003; Mendelson-Forman 2006). Clearly there could have been better coordination of the technical aspects of reform (particularly on coordination of criminal justice institutions of the police, courts, and prisons), but the major failing of these efforts was the inability or unwillingness to tackle the political dimension of institutional reform. To have any prospect of success, current efforts will require strong safeguards against political interference in and corruption of this key state institution.

Justice and the Rule of Law

The rule of law is not only essential to ensuring security and justice; it also creates an enabling environment for investments, economic growth, empowerment of the poor, and development. According to the Interim Cooperation Framework Summary Report (2004),

---

93. This admission was made in the context of the prosecution of 15 police officers for their roles in the August 20, 2005, attack on a football stadium in Martissant, in which at least six civilians were killed (Associated Press, November 10, 2005).

94. UN Security Council Resolution 1542, April 30, 2004 (S/RES/1542).

95. See Refugees International (RI) statement released March 2005, entitled "Haiti: UN Civilian Police Require Executive Authority."

96. UN Security Council Resolution 1608, June 22, 2005 (S/RES/1608).

97. Report of the Secretary-General on the United Nations Stabilization Mission in Haiti, May 13, 2005, (S/2005/313), paragraphs 22–25.

weaknesses in respect for the law and basic liberties have led to corruption, insecurity and impunity, and have discouraged productive investments by the private sector. A recent assessment for the UN finds a broad range of deficiencies in Haiti's judicial institutions and suggests that respect for the rule of law has fallen to its lowest point since 1994 (ILAC 2005). Haiti's legal institutions are beset by the advanced deterioration of their physical infrastructure, the obsolescence of many laws, the absence of basic guarantees, politicization, corruption, and drug smuggling. As a result, "access to law and justice remains difficult and random" (ICF 2004) despite a decade in which donors provided significant financial and technical assistance to reform the country's legal institutions. Why has this effort failed? Numerous assessments have identified the multiple dysfunctions in the administration of justice, the protection of human rights, and the rule of law in Haiti (O'Neill 1995; Barthelemy and others 1999; ILAC 2005). Clearly, it has not been possible to "fix" justice in Haiti through international assistance alone. This section examines the challenges to justice in Haiti, reviews lessons learned from previous justice reform efforts, and considers current challenges for reform.

Judicial Independence and Accountability

The independence of the judiciary is guaranteed under the 1987 constitution, which sets varying periods of tenure for judges. Judges are to be appointed by the president on the basis of lists prepared by the Senate (for the Supreme Court and five Appeals Courts) and by Departmental and Communal Assemblies for 15 first instance courts (*Tribunaux de première instance*) and about 200 peace courts (*Tribunaux de paix*). In practice, however, the judiciary is subordinate to the executive and the minister of justice controls the judicial budget, as well as the training, appointment, and dismissal of judges.

At the lowest level of the justice system, justices of the peace (*Juges de paix*) have a broad range of functions in civil, criminal, and extrajudicial matters. They issue warrants, adjudicate minor infractions, mediate cases, take depositions, and refer cases to prosecutors or higher judicial officials. Investigating magistrates and public prosecutors cooperate in more serious cases, which are tried by the judges of the first instance courts. Appeals court judges hear cases referred from the first instance courts, and the Supreme Court (*Cour de Cassation*) deals with questions of procedure and constitutionality.

Judges are underpaid, have limited or no access to legal texts, and have little opportunity for professional development. More than half of the justices of the peace have no law degree, and many exercise an expanded and arbitrary jurisdiction over criminal matters (ILAC 2005). Thus, while many magistrates struggle to administer justice under extremely difficult conditions, lack of training, inadequate pay, and political pressures result in serious problems of corruption for which there are no effective accountability mechanisms.[98] Despite a number of qualified and experienced jurists, "judicial and professional independence remains a priority" (ILAC 2005).

The ICF Sectoral Report on Justice, Prisons and Human Rights (2004) notes that the ministry of justice suffers from a "paralysis of disorganization and dysfunction" as a result

---

98. The National Association of Haitian Magistrates (ANAMAH) was created in January 2002, and in 2003 adopted a Code of Ethics for Haitian judges. However, this remains a voluntary code of conduct.

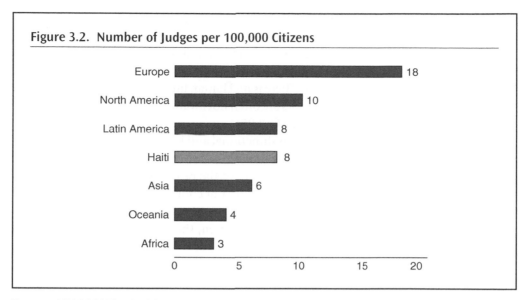

Figure 3.2. Number of Judges per 100,000 Citizens

Region	Judges
Europe	18
North America	10
Latin America	8
Haiti	8
Asia	6
Oceania	4
Africa	3

Sources: ICLAC 2005/UNODC 2005.

of weak management, administration, budgets, procurement, logistics, and personnel policy.[99] With 600 judges, including 375 justices of the peace (GOH 2004), in 2002 the size of Haiti's judiciary relative to population was in line with regional averages at eight judges per 100,000 citizens (Figure 3.2). The ministry, however, has limited ability to oversee the proper functioning of the court system and lacks the capacity to gather and analyze statistics on performance indicators and outcomes.

The court system's physical infrastructure is also weak. It had been in a general state of disrepair before the disturbances of 2004, when it largely collapsed. The ICF reports that 10 of 16 courts of first instance and several peace courts were destroyed.[100] Court records are poor, case filing systems are weak, and court documents are often lost.

Access to Justice

Most of Haiti's population is effectively excluded from the formal justice system. The territorial coverage of the first level of formal justice through peace courts is uneven, and many were destroyed or fell into a state of disrepair following the violent uprisings of 2004. As a result of a dysfunctional civil registry (*état civile*), 40 percent of Haitians lack the basic civil identity documentation necessary to secure legal standing before the court.[101] Most legal proceedings are conducted and court documents are in French, although most of the population understands only Creole. There is no public defender's office or any systematic

99. CCI Groupe Thématique: Securité et Gouvernance Politique; Sous-Groupe: Justice – Prisons – Droits Humains, 16 juin, p.3.

100. Ibid. p.3.

101. Proposals for the transfer of the voter registration system of identity cards established for 2006 national elections into the permanent civil registry could significantly improve this situation.

provision of legal assistance (ILAC 2005). Most Haitians cannot afford a lawyer and the state is not required to provide one.

The country's legal codes need radical overhaul.[102] The judicial apparatus follows a civil law system based on the Napoleonic Code. The criminal code dates from 1832, although it has been amended in some instances. There is no Haitian literature on jurisprudence and ILAC reports that "judges and prosecutors are often not aware that a law has been repealed, key laws adopted or a treaty ratified" (ILAC 2005).

Because the formal justice system is dysfunctional and inaccessible, many matters are resolved through customary law and other informal mechanisms. Customary norms influence the formal law practiced by the justices of the peace, who deal with more than 80 percent of the cases in Haiti. Customary laws are not codified or reflected in the official legal system—and thus cannot be reviewed by the formal system—and there are no safeguards to ensure the protection of the rights of women, the poor, or other marginalized groups (ILAC 2005).

The Criminal Justice System

The judiciary, police, and prisons are under the administrative oversight of the minister of justice but these institutions are only partially integrated into a functioning criminal justice system or *chaîne pénale*. There are long delays in the administration of justice because of communication failures between the investigative "judicial" police and prosecutors on evidence-gathering and the preparation of cases, inadequate tracking and management of case files by court clerks, and deficient enforcement of judicial orders for prisoner transfers and release. To lower the rates of pretrial detention and combat impunity for criminal activities, it is essential to improve the functioning of the criminal justice system through capacity-building of each institution and to enhance coordination among the various institutional actors (the police, judiciary and prisons) so that they can process criminal cases through the system.

Before the National Penitentiary Administration (APENA) was created in 1995, prisons were administered by the military and were largely beyond judicial oversight. APENA was created as Haiti's first civilian corrections system and had to be built from scratch. A June 1997 presidential decree placed it under the authority of the HNP. Since then it has become the Department for Penitentiary Administration and manages 21 corrections facilities with capacity for about 3,800 detainees, 1,600 of whom are in Port-au-Prince (ICF 2004). During the violent unrest of 2004, however, angry mobs vented their frustration against state authorities by attacking police stations and prisons, destroying infrastructures and releasing most of the detainees.

Between 1995 and 2004, there were improvements in the sanitary, medical, and basic nutritional conditions of detention. The management of correction facilities and personnel also improved, as did record-keeping on detainees (UNDP 2003). Yet, because of delays

---

102. Significant international assistance has been provided for the reform of legal code, but these have remained largely on paper and will require a functioning legislature to be enacted.

in the criminal justice process, as many as 80 percent of detainees remain in preventive detention; some wait several months, if not years, before they are brought before a judge. Several human rights groups have criticized the high levels of pretrial detention in Haiti, and a significant proportion of cases are considered to be examples of "prolonged pretrial detention" (Vera Institute of Justice 2002). Violations of prisoners' human rights are a major concern, particularly in police lockups, where suspects are detained before being transferred to the corrections authorities.[103]

Lessons Learned 1994–2004

International engagement in the justice sector began with the joint OAS/UN International Civilian Mission in Haiti (MICIVIH), which was established in 1993 during the military rule of General Cedras and continued through a successive series of UN missions after President Aristide's return in 1994. The United States, Canada, France, and the European Union all provided significant bilateral assistance throughout the 1990s.

During this period, a substantial amount of bilateral aid went into the construction and functioning of the courts—particularly local "peace courts," first instance courts, and prosecutors offices—throughout Haiti. Efforts were made to reform the country's outdated legal system: the National Preparatory Commission for Legal and Justice Reform was established in 1997 and was followed by the National Commission for the Reform of Legal Codes. Both of these received significant technical assistance. The reform process largely stalled, however, because there was no functioning legislature and the process lacked political support.

The Magistrates School (*Ecole de la Magistrature*, EMA) received substantial donor support following its creation in 1995 and several hundred judges and court officials were trained in Haiti and abroad. But its legal basis (organic law) was never secured. By 2004 it had stopped functioning and had become the unofficial headquarters of the former military (ILAC 2005). The ministry of justice received administrative and technical support, while APENA was given assistance for the rehabilitation and professionalization of the corrections system. The Ombudsman's Office (*Office du Protecteur du Citoyen*) also received some modest support.

Some areas within each institution changed for the better but there has been limited evidence of an improvement in the overall functioning of the justice sector. In May 1999, despite successive UN missions with mandates to support reform, the secretary general reported that overall little progress had been made in reforming the justice system and that major structural weakness continued to undermine the rule of law and civil liberties.[104]

In 2000, following a critical evaluation of the impact of justice reform programs, The U.S. Agency for International Development (USAID) reoriented its entire justice program towards civil society and the NGO sector. As the electoral disputes of 2000 developed into

---

103. The Haitian National Human Rights Defense Network (RNDDH) documents human rights violations of individuals in police custody and prison conditions. See reports online at http://www.rnddh.org.
104. Report of the Secretary-General on the United Nations Civilian Police Mission in Haiti, May 19, 1999, S/1999/579.

a broader political and economic crisis, the UN system and other bilateral donors reduced their levels of technical and financial assistance for reform. From 2000 onwards, these efforts were increasingly undermined by growing levels of political interference, corruption, and polarization between government and civil society.

After 2000, the government's interference in the legal process escalated. There was blatant interference in several high profile cases, including the investigation of the murder of the well-known journalist Jean Dominique. Government officials threatened and pressured a number of judges working on Dominique's case, many were dismissed, and others fled to exile (ICG 2004). In 2003, the Inter-American Commission on Human Rights (IACHR) reported that judges and magistrates have been pressured by the authorities, gangs, or violent and sometimes armed groups seeking to influence the outcome of certain cases, particularly when they are dealing with politically charged matters.[105]

The problems of corruption and political interference that plagued the police and judiciary also undermined prison reform. A riot in 2001 resulted in the partial destruction of the national penitentiary in Port-au-Prince and the escape of a number of individuals detained on drug trafficking charges. In 2002, former Aristide loyalist and gang leader Amayot Metayer, who was suspected of directing attacks on the opposition, was arrested and flown by helicopter to the national penitentiary but then returned to prison in Gonaive where he, along with over 100 fellow inmates, was liberated by his "Cannibal Army" supporters in rioting that left the prison facility largely destroyed. After a public reconciliation with President Aristide and intimidation of an investigating judge to "legalize" his release, Metayer was murdered (Deibert 2005).

During the post-2004 transition, international observers have expressed increasing concern about the lack of due process against former government officials and Lavalas supporters, including former Prime Minister Yvon Neptune and activist Father Jean Juste, who have been subjected to long-term "preventive detention" involving extended delays in presenting formal charges (Amnesty International 2005). The quick acquittal of people previously convicted of human rights abuses—notably some ex-leaders of the Front for the Advancement and Progress of Haiti (FRAPH), who also led the uprising against President Aristide[106] —has also prompted concern (ICG 2004). Following an official visit to Haiti in September 2004, the IACHR (2004) pointed to "failures on the part of authorities in Haiti to effectively investigate, prosecute and punish serious violations of human rights, as well as claims that criminal proceedings have been undertaken for inappropriate and political purposes."

A 2003 evaluation of rule of law programs in Haiti by the United Nations Development Programme concludes that a decade of concentrated donor assistance was insufficient to ensure justice reform and the rule of law in a poor country with fragile democratic institutions (UNDP 2003). The report suggests that the international community shares some of the responsibility for the failure because of its overly optimistic presumption that high levels of external resources and concentrated international expertise—with little consideration

---

105. IACHR, press release no. 24/03 (August 22, 2003):http://www.cidh.org/Comunicados/English/2003/24.03.htm.

106. Louis Jodel Chamblain (former leader of FRAPH) was convicted in absentia for the murder of a prominent Lavalas supporters in 1993. In February 2004, he was among the leaders of the uprising against Aristide. On August 16, 2004, he was acquitted for the 1993 murder after a one-day trial (ICG 2004).

of absorptive capacity or assessment of the real interest in change—could quickly transform a nation. Furthermore, many international programs were based on assessments that listed the many dysfunctions of the justice system rather than offering a strategic analysis of how to support system-wide transformation. As a result, many donors undertook relatively unproblematic interventions that addressed particular technical needs (Barthelemy 1999). Finally, international assistance programs also underestimated the political dimension of justice reform, which faced resistance from powerful sectors in Haiti that had traditionally been able to "buy" justice. Too much of the international community's expectations for reform were dependent on the goodwill of the minister of justice, of whom there were 10 between 1994 and 2004[107] (Tremblay 2004).

Following the establishment of an Interim Government in 2004, national and international experts engaged in the preparation of a joint needs assessment and planning exercise that included the justice sector. The resulting ICF identifies a number of priorities for the sector, including: reducing impunity by strengthening the criminal process and updating the criminal procedure code; strengthening judicial independence; rehabilitating court infrastructures; providing legal training and information for judicial personnel; increasing access to justice by providing legal assistance and promoting alternative means of dispute-settlement and mediation; and fostering women's participation in the provision of justice (ICF 2004). This broad range of actions, however, lacks a clear order of priorities and performance measures, has received little financing and, according to implementation reports, has had mixed results.[108]

Practical and strategic lessons have been learned from a decade of frustrated efforts to reform the police and the justice system in Haiti. Chief among these is that the reforms cannot be reduced to technical capacity building, training, and infrastructure, but instead must be integrated into a broader process of state building and democratic consolidation. Institution building requires a long-term engagement by national and international actors. The creation of a national constituency in favor of reform is essential to furthering change in the police and justice system. Future efforts will have to balance support for the institutional "supply" of the administration of justice and police with a strengthening of the "demand" for justice. Civil society-led initiatives, such as the *Forum Citoyen* (Citizen's Forum) and the Haiti Coalition for the Reform of Law and Justice, seek to engage a broad range of local and national stakeholders in devising proposals for reform. The demand for reform will remain frustrated, however, unless it has political support across the judicial, legislative, and executive branches of government, and unless corruption and political interference in the legal process ends.

Conclusion: Restoring the Capacity of State Institutions

This chapter has considered the state's ability to provide basic public goods in Haiti and finds that ability to be very limited as a result of decades of neglect, political capture and corruption. As regards the state's administrative capacity, the territorial reach of state

---

107. The Minister of Justice, Jean-Baptiste Brown, resigned in 2003, citing obstacles to the reform of the police and judiciary (Deibert, 250).

108. Daniel Dorsainvil, Rapport d'Evaluation de la Mise en Oeuvre du Cadre de Cooperation Interimaire, septembre 2005 et octobre 2005.

institutions is minimal outside major urban centers, decentralization has not been implemented, and the state has been unable to provide basic services or infrastructures to large portions of the population. A diverse and vibrant non-state sector has filled some of the gaps in health and education, but these efforts have been largely uncoordinated and unregulated. The result has been a substantial variation in the quality of the services provided and significant gaps in services for certain regions and vulnerable groups. The institutions responsible for providing the essential public goods of security and the rule of law (namely, the police and judiciary) are largely ineffective and suffer repeated problems of political interference and corruption.

The state's limited capacity to provide these core public goods of basic services, security, and the rule of law constitutes the second "institutional" dimension of the poverty-conflict trap that has thwarted development efforts in Haiti. Our analysis has shown that Haiti's institutions are unable to mitigate the significant demographic and socioeconomic problems that the country faces as a result of its long-term development crisis. Without direct international support, the state cannot control the violence and insecurity that spring from political mobilization or criminal manipulation of grievances. The weakness of mechanisms for institutional accountability makes the public sector vulnerable to political capture and corruption, which further undermines the ability of institutions to mitigate socioeconomic risks. Having established that political and social actors are largely unconstrained by the institutional context, the next chapter analyzes the strategies and objectives of political actors in Haiti.

CHAPTER 4

Political Forces and Actors

*By Dan Erikson, Emma Grant, Franka Braun,
Gillette Hall, Katherine Bain, Mark Mattner,
Stephanie Kuttner, and Willy Egset*

This chapter addresses the third set of "political" factors that contribute to Haiti's conflict-poverty trap. Twenty years have passed since the 1986 ouster of Jean-Claude "Baby Doc" Duvalier created a window of opportunity to establish a more stable and democratic form of governance. Haiti's highly polarized politics, however, have complicated efforts to address the country's complex and deeply rooted development challenges. After decades of dictatorship, Haiti's democratic leaders inherited a country whose potential had been wasted and underdeveloped for generations, and faced the tremendous challenge of undertaking economic and political development with limited resources. This called for extraordinary leadership, but the opportunities of the post-authoritarian period have been squandered as the country's citizens have suffered the effects of continuing political confrontation, faltering democratic institutions, and the collapse of the state security apparatus amid surging crime and violence—circumstances that have led to repeated international interventions. This chapter analyzes the use of political violence in Haiti before and after the democratic transition, with a view to understanding the underlying forces and dynamics that perpetuate conflict. It looks at how "entrepreneurs of violence" have corrupted some of the country's popular movements as a political strategy, and considers the extent to which elections and democratic institutions serve as checks and balances in Haiti's troubled political process.

A History of Political Violence

Political violence is not new in Haiti's history. It neither started nor ended with the Duvalier regime, although the regime's record of violent repression is unmatched. "Papa Doc" Duvalier began to institutionalize political violence soon after he was elected in 1957, by establishing a force of *cagoulards* ("hooded men"). These were charged with silencing supporters of rival candidates who challenged the election results, and they gradually developed into an extensive network of spies for the regime. In 1962, the *cagoulards* were formalized into the *Volontaires de la Sécurité Nationale* (VSN), commonly known as the *Tontons Macoutes* (the bogeymen),[109] a loosely organized and generally unpaid nationwide militia of at least 12,000 members, which became the most powerful of the various military and paramilitary organizations created by Duvalier.[110] The VSN neutralized political opposition, including the church, the urban business community, student organizations, and trade unions. Crucially, it was also a means to subdue the national army, the country's traditional kingmaker, and to recruit supporters of the regime nationwide (Nicholls 1996; Heinl and Heinl 1978). Duvalier's violence was not limited to political targets: children, women, whole families, and even whole villages or neighborhoods could be targeted. The exact number of those killed during his government is uncertain. Human Rights Watch estimates 20,000 to 30,000 civilian deaths during both Duvalier regimes (1957–86) (HRW 1996), while other sources estimate that 50,000 were killed during "Papa Doc's" 14-year reign alone (Laguerre 1994).

"Baby Doc" Duvalier fled Haiti on February 7, 1986, never to be held accountable for the atrocities committed under his or his father's regime. In Haiti, however, a vigilante campaign of *dechoukage* ("uprooting") led to the killing of an unknown number of *macoutes* and other supporters of the old regime. Yet the *macoutes*, though disbanded, were neither disarmed nor prosecuted, since the National Governing Council (CNG) and subsequent cabinets between 1987 and the 1990 elections were led mostly by army officers from the Duvalier era. *L'insécurité*—a term used to describe the fear of arbitrary violence spreading at the time—was also caused by the *zenglendos*, armed and violent gangs (including former *macoutes*) that spread in this period. The army claimed to represent a break with the past but on April 26, 1986, troops opened fire on a crowd commemorating victims of the Duvalier regime, killing eight people. In similar incidents that were intended to undermine support for democratic candidates in the planned elections, the army attacked demonstrators, literacy program and democracy activists, peasant organizations, church groups, and poor neighborhoods where the opposition to military rule was most intense.[111]

After a brief civilian interregnum, a coup brought General Namphy to power in June 1988. Under his rule the severe persecution of democracy activists continued, culminating in an attack on the Church of St. Jean Bosco during Father Aristide's sermon on September 11, 1998, an incident in which at least a dozen unarmed churchgoers were killed.[112] The event

---

109. The organization was also a vehicle to garner backing and create loyalty among Duvalier's support base, the black middle and lower middle class, which initially represented the typical VSN members.

110. Other armed units included the Presidential Guard, the *Casernes Dessalines*, the "*Leopards*," the police (part of the army), and the national army (FA'dH) itself. The courts and prisons were also important tools for Duvalier. In rural areas, the *chefs de sections* (typically also members of the VSN) ruled Haiti's 565 rural sections (municipal subdivisions) violently (Human Rights Watch 1996).

111. Two infamous massacres occurred during this period. In the northwestern town of Jean Rabel on July 23, 1987, an estimated 139 peasants were killed by gangs paid by large landowners to offset land redistribution demands. And in the Election Day massacre on November 29, 1987, 34 voters and election workers were killed by army-affiliated thugs (HRW 1996).

112. Aristide barely escaped and the incident made him the pivotal figure in the democratic movement, a symbolic leader of the poor and oppressed. Many invested him with mythical and mystical powers because of his escape (Fatton 2002).

turned even soldiers against the regime and eventually paved the way for a civilian interim president (Trouillot) who oversaw the organization of elections in December 1990, when Aristide was elected with two-thirds of the votes.[113]

Not even the rampant violence between 1986 and 1991, however, matched the severe terror launched by the military coup of September 30, 1991—a terror that continued until President Aristide's return in 1994. According to Human Rights Watch, 1,000 people were killed in just the first month after the coup, and an estimated 2,000–3,000 more were killed in political violence orchestrated by the military junta over the next three years. Many thousands more suffered "disappearance," torture, beatings, rape, and arbitrary detention. About 100,000 fled the country, while 300,000 went into internal exile (HRW 1996). The objective, according to a contemporary report, was to "systematically . . . eviscerate all civic, popular and professional organizations opposed to [the government's] authoritarian rule" (HRW 1993). The violence was perpetrated by the army and also by the *attachés*, armed civilian members of the FRAPH.[114] The *attachés* operated almost exclusively in urban areas, in the popular neighborhoods and the slums, targeting the Cité Soleil area in particular, where they terrorized the general population and those suspected of being Aristide supporters, driving many to internal exile in rural areas (Corten 2000). International reactions were muted and focused on finding a negotiated solution. The agreement brokered with the coup leaders by U.S. negotiators on September 18, 1994, included a general amnesty for crimes against individuals as well as against the state. Again, some supporters of the coup were subjected to vigilante violence rather than judicial process: 45 people were killed in March 1995 and eight in November, while the coup leaders went into exile. Only limited progress was later made in investigating and prosecuting some of the worst atrocities.

A Difficult Democratic Transition, 1990–2004

The fragmentation and turbulent nature of Haiti's political party system is closely linked to the failure of democratic and institutional consolidation since the fall of Duvalier. In the past two decades the democratic process has been repeatedly interrupted and undermined— initially by remnants of the Duvalier regime, later by conflicts among former democratic allies, and most recently by armed groups of various political leanings. Today, Haiti's party system remains highly fragmented and few political forces express themselves through regular party structures. Official political parties are generally small and narrowly based, led by figures of varying stature and charisma.

Political parties have played an evolving role since the elections of December 1990 that brought about Haiti's initial democratic triumph after years of popular mobilization and

---

113. A failed coup in January 1991 triggered reprisal killings of at least 30 suspected coup supporters. Investigations into these atrocities and institutional reform to prevent them from occurring again started haltingly during Aristide's first tenure from February 7 to September 30, 1991, but vigilante violence continued. According to Human Rights Watch, none of these killings was ordered by Aristide but "the president never threw his considerable moral authority behind [a] condemnation. Indeed, at times, Aristide seemed to endorse the threat of vigilante violence as a legitimate political tool" (HRW 1996).

114. Front pour l'Avancement et le Progrès d'Haïti. The acronym played on the French verb "frapper," to hit or strike.

severe military repression. President Aristide, who rose to prominence as the voice of the democratic movement, won with 67 percent of the vote because of support from the urban and rural poor. Accepting the leadership of Lavalas, a coalition of the popular movement that brought together the poor and anti-Duvalierist forces, Aristide sought to advance the representation of the poor through elections but left little room for internal dissent. This alliance helped put down the first coup attempt against him in January 1991 and later he relied on popular mobilization rather than institutional reform when confronted with opposition from the army and the economic elite. The movement's strength, however, was overestimated: seven months later the army crushed the democratic government and its supporters in an exceptionally brutal coup. Since then, however, popular mobilization outside regular institutional channels has become central to wielding power in Haiti.

After President Aristide's restoration to the Haitian National Palace in October 1994, the pro-Aristide coalition led by the *Organisation Politique Lavalas* (OPL) swept the nationwide local and parliamentary elections in June 1995. But President Aristide's reluctance to step down at the end of his term in December 1995 opened a breach in the OPL between Aristide loyalists and an independent social democratic wing. This power struggle culminated in a split in November 1996, when Aristide withdrew from the OPL and formed the Fanmi Lavalas. Fanmi Lavalas benefited from the social constituency Aristide had built and the support he enjoyed among the poorer sections of the population. In 1997, the two parties ran against each other in attempted legislative elections, which were aborted because of new allegations of fraud. That marked the start of a political stalemate between the presidency, controlled by Fanmi Lavalas, and the legislature, dominated by the OPL, an impasse that prevented the appointment of a cabinet and hindered access to international aid (Dailey 2003).

The May 2000 elections marked a new shift in Haiti's political system. They followed a period of almost 18 months in which President Préval ruled by decree after legislators' terms expired and parliament was dissolved. After repeated delays, new nationwide elections on all levels took place on May 21 and the main opposition parties formed a coalition called the *Espace de Concertation*. The electoral process, however, collapsed amid allegations of fraud and irregular ballot-counting procedures that favored government-supported Lavalas candidates. International observers, led by the OAS, withheld their endorsement of the elections and the major opposition parties withdrew, leaving Lavalas entirely in control of the legislative branch. In November 2000, Aristide won the presidency with 92 per cent of the vote in an election boycotted by the opposition. There were sharp disputes about the level of voter turnout: the government and some of its supporters claimed 60 percent participation, while other observers put the figure at 10 percent or less. Aristide therefore re-emerged as the dominant political force in circumstances that called his legitimacy into question.

A series of international initiatives to resolve the stalemate were unsuccessful, as an increasingly authoritarian government faced an opposition that was ever more determined to depose President Aristide. The 2000–2004 period was characterized by fitful and unproductive negotiations between President Aristide's Lavalas government and members of the opposition coalition that formed to protest the election. The legislative and municipal elections of May 2000 were intended to resolve the political crisis by restoring a democratically elected parliament. Instead, they compounded the problem and set the stage for a prolonged stalemate between the ruling Fanmi Lavalas party and the coalition of opposition parties known as the *Convergence Democratique*.

Political Mobilization and Entrepreneurs of Violence

The strength of the popular mobilization against Duvalier's authoritarian regime was provided by a broad and diverse collection of groups commonly known as the *Organisations Populaires* (OPs). The movement included peasant organizations, student groups, labor unions, and neighborhood committees in poor urban areas. These neighborhood committees mobilized to demand services such as potable water and electricity, to defend their neighborhoods from crime and violence, and to organize themselves politically (Aristide and Richardson 1994).

During the 1990s, the leaders of some OPs had begun to seek public sector jobs, using control over their organization and their militant credentials as bargaining chips. At the same time, frustrations with the democratic process and the allocation of small assistance projects made the organizations susceptible to political cooptation. Gradually, some OPs came to serve as political tools for Lavalas—particularly in slum areas—in exchange for jobs, projects, or impunity for criminal activities. The OPs increasingly exercised control over neighborhoods from which the state was generally absent, by providing services and security. More directly, OP leaders and members were offered positions in the public administration or public enterprises, thus receiving incomes and exerting political control (Lafontante 2003).

The political impasse and subsequent deterioration in the 1990s transformed some parts of this movement into violent government enforcers and criminal groups. As with the *macoutes* under Duvalier, the military junta's *attachés*, and the *zenglendos* of the early 1990s, some OPs became the *chimeres* (armed gangs) of an increasingly militarized Lavalas, serving as the government's private and violent enforcers (Fatton 2002; ICG 2004).[115] This continuity among the parallel forces of state violence stems partly from competition for scarce resources, as well as allegiance to politically powerful personalities.[116]

In July 2001, former FAd'H soldiers attacked police stations in Port-au-Prince and in some provinces, triggering government reprisals against opposition parties that had formed the *Convergence Démocratique* coalition.[117] The National Palace was similarly attacked in December 2001, followed by *chimere* attacks on offices and residences of opposition politicians and the killing of one opposition activist (ICG 2004).

Throughout 2002 and 2003, the political crisis deepened and violence escalated. According to international observers, the police were withdrawn from some urban areas

---

115. This representation of the transformation of some segments of the OPs was confirmed by several knowledgeable sources in Haiti in personal interviews in Port-au-Prince during May 2005, including with two prominent Haitian journalists.

116. One of the pro-Aristide gang leaders of Cité Soleil reportedly declared that "we are the sons of the macoutes." (Diederich 2005).

117. The Convergence comprised about 20 political parties, from right to left, united in their opposition to Aristide but with no joint political program.

to allow militant OP gangs to break up opposition rallies and to attack opposition politicians, human rights activists, journalists, and others (ICG 2004; Amnesty International 2004). Among the most lethal incidents in this escalating low-intensity war between the Lavalas regime (a war waged by its police forces, with the support of armed militants) and anti-Lavalas gangs were two battles between the police and the "Cannibal Army" over the strategically important city of Gonaïves, first in October 2003 and later in February 2004. In both incidents at least "a dozen" individuals died in battle and as a result of revenge killings. In another incident, which is now under investigation, the police and pro-government gangs allegedly killed about 20 people linked with opposition parties on February 9–10, 2004, in St. Marc (ICG 2004).

Other political groups have become aware of the importance of control in the populous poor neighborhoods. According to some reports, shortly after President Aristide's departure in 2004 the political opposition (Groupe 184) met gang leaders in Cité Soleil to ask for the gangs' disarmament (Griffin 2004). One of the most critical challenges for the new government will be the violent potential of urban gangs, some of which are linked to grassroots elements of the Lavalas movement. In the absence of economic opportunities or increased social benefits, the Haitian government will have to find ways to respond to the grievances of these popular groups in order to maintain some level of social peace.

Other armed groups continue to operate outside the legal political arena. These include the Ex-FAd'H, some 2,300 members of the former army (plus new recruits) who have maintained an informal organization since 1995 and who now demand back-payment of salaries and pensions, as well as other forms of economic support, including jobs in the national police force. Most of the Ex-FAd'H have been willing to join the disarmament and reintegration program supervised by the government's demobilization office, but dissatisfaction with the program's effectiveness has been growing. The Ex-FAd'H is not a strong force today but is probably about as strong as it was in 2004, and recently it has attacked UN peacekeepers and police stations in the North Department. Other armed groups have carried out sporadic attacks on public facilities in remote areas. In June 2005, for example, an allegedly communist group known as the Dessalines National Liberation Army attacked a police station and voting center in the northern town of Le Borgne.

Checks and Balances in Haiti's Political Process

Historically, Haiti's problems of political governance have not been solved through elections, which have repeatedly been marked by irregularities, intimidation, and violence. Even this year's presidential election, which was characterized by peaceful voting and the participation of an estimated 2.2 million of the country's 3.5 million voters, was complicated by allegations of fraud and massive street demonstrations while the losing candidates challenged the legitimacy of the result. Indeed, the very fact that 33 candidates chose to contest the presidency reveals the country's high level of political fragmentation, although the robust support for a single candidate (Préval) demonstrates that the vast majority of Haiti's poor are not nearly as divided as the country's elites. This broad base of support and international recognition of the election results creates an important opportunity for partnership between donors, government, and civil society to address Haiti's multifaceted development challenges.

The 2006 elections were an important first step but they do not ensure national reconciliation, and Haiti is likely to face enduring challenges of political polarization during the next five years. While efforts persist to find a new social contract or a viable political compromise, international development agencies should seek to prioritize areas in which there are already elements of political consensus, such as in health, education, infrastructure, electricity, sanitation, as well as security and the rule of law. By supporting efforts at political dialogue and by focusing on the provision of basic services, development assistance may contribute to greater democratic stability in Haiti.

Traditionally, Haiti has had a strong presidential system wherein the president holds the seat of power and does not submit to the normal checks and balances that accompany the democratic process. The 1987 constitution stipulates that the executive, legislature, and judiciary are three co-equal branches of government. As discussed in the previous section on governance and institutions, the judiciary is independent only in theory because it is administratively and politically dependent on the executive branch through the minister of justice. The legislative branch consists of two representative houses: the Chamber of Deputies with 99 seats and the Senate with 30. Constitutionally, parliament is supposed to play a crucial role in governing the country by naming a prime minister, adopting the government's budget, and overseeing the operation of the ministries and the cabinet. However, the parliament lacks a working committee structure, a professional staff, or even adequate physical facilities.

The constitution establishes a complex mechanism for the balancing of state power through political decentralization to regional departments and local communes, but this procedure has not been implemented (see the discussion in the previous section on governance and institutions). The indefinite postponement of local elections for the 420 local executive positions (a mayor and two deputies for each municipality) and 9,000 community officials has prompted concern that many local positions will remain vacant or be filled by central government appointees. According to the "bottom-up" democratic mechanisms of the Haitian constitution, local elections are required for the establishment of a permanent electoral council, which has yet to be put in place. Its absence has required the establishment of a series of interim electoral councils whose legitimacy and effectiveness has been repeatedly undermined by infighting and political crises over the appointment of members. The establishment of a credible permanent electoral body will be crucial in supporting the consolidation of democracy in Haiti.

In practice, Haiti's political structure lacks a predictable system of rules and it will be very difficult to achieve lasting stability without establishing an equilibrium among the competing forces within society. Historically, the small elite has been pitted against the vastly larger urban and rural poor. Haitian politics swing between two key dangers: capture by privileged elites who harness government to protect their dominant position in society; and populism that neglects the country's long-term institutional and economic development while paying lip service to the poor. If a balance can be struck between the contending social forces, Haiti's return to elected rule may allow for a new period of democratic consolidation.

Conclusion: Strong National Leadership is Crucial
to Breaking the Conflict-Poverty Trap

This chapter has considered the role of political actors and forces in explaining Haiti's conflict-poverty trap. It has reviewed the legacy of political violence that has evolved from earlier periods of dictatorship and military repression into decentralized and localized power struggles, particularly in the urban slums. These circumstances have created opportunities for entrepreneurs of violence to manipulate popular grievances for political and criminal ends in a situation where the formal political process and public institutions provide only weak checks and balances. Breaking free of Haiti's poverty-conflict trap will require capable national political leadership that is committed to the consolidation of democratic institutions and processes. In a context of very difficult socioeconomic conditions, immense social risks, defunct state institutions, extremely limited budget resources, and political polarization, Haiti's leaders face enormous challenges. The 2006 electoral process, however, has created new opportunities for reform, reconciliation and partnerships.

CHAPTER 5

Conclusion: Breaking Out of the Conflict-Poverty Trap

By Dorte Verner, Stephanie Kuttner,
and Willy Egset

Haiti is a resilient society whose rural communities in particular have developed coping mechanisms in response to a long history of underdevelopment and poor governance. Like other fragile states, however, Haiti is beset by widespread poverty and inequality, economic decline and unemployment, institutional weakness and corruption, violence, lawlessness, and recurrent conflict. Nonetheless, while violent conflicts are concentrated in poor countries, poverty alone does not *cause* conflict. In most cases, violent conflict is a symptom of multifaceted development and governance malfunctions and it also reinforces those malfunctions. This is the logic of a conflict-poverty trap that has been the analytical framework for this study.

This report has examined Haiti's conflict-poverty trap from the perspective of the triangle of factors that have been identified as the main components of such traps, including (a) demographic and socioeconomic factors at the individual and household levels; (b) the capacity of the state to provide public goods, including security and the rule of law; and (c) the agendas and strategies of political actors in facing these challenges. In its three main chapters, the report has explored the nature of these three components and assessed the extent to which they exacerbate or mitigate conflict and poverty risks. This conclusion draws together the results of the main chapters in an analysis of the interaction between different risk factors. The figure below presents a simplified illustration of interactions in the triangle of interdependent risk factors that perpetuate the conflict-poverty cycle in Haiti.

Haiti's poverty-conflict trap is fuelled by demographic and socioeconomic outcomes of widespread poverty and inequality, rapid urbanization, and high youth unemployment. These result in high social risks and demands on weak state institutions for basic services.

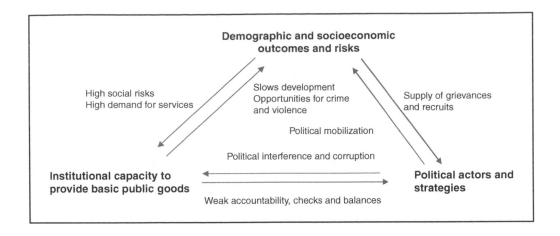

Poor governance and the state's inability to provide public goods such as security, infrastructure, and basic services in turn undermine development and poverty reduction, thus exacerbating negative demographic and socioeconomic outcomes. Weakened by corruption and political interference, the police and judiciary are unable to manage the negative social outcomes of crime and violence, particularly in urban areas. As a result, there is a steady stream of grievances and disaffected youth who can be recruited by "entrepreneurs of violence" for criminal activities and political mobilization. Competition for control of lucrative transshipment routes for the illegal drugs trade further compounds these problems. Institutions cannot provide the checks and balances necessary for the peaceful resolution of conflicting interests, and instead some political actors resort to illegal and violent methods. The weakness of accountability mechanisms within state institutions creates opportunities for political interference and corruption, further weakening those institutions and thereby perpetuating the conflict-poverty cycle. The sections below explore the interactions between these different factors in more detail, and suggest entry points for reconstruction and development strategies to address them.

Widespread Poverty and Inequality, Rapid Urbanization, and High Youth Unemployment Increase the Risks of Crime and Conflict

Research shows that, among economic risk factors, inequality appears to be a crucial element in increasing crime (both violent and other), while poverty is linked to increased risk of violent conflict. Unfortunately, Haiti suffers both from high rates of poverty (nearly half of households are trapped in absolute poverty and live on less than a dollar a day) and highly inequitable income distribution (it has one of the world's highest Gini coefficients, at 0.66). Social indicators such as literacy, life expectancy, infant mortality, and child malnutrition show that poverty is also extensive in Haiti, although most non-income poverty indicators have been improving. Domestic migration and education reduce the likelihood of falling into poverty, but access to assets such as education, infrastructure, and basic services is highly unequal and strongly associated with poverty.

Haiti's enormous social and economic inequalities reflect a history of development neglect of secondary cities and rural areas since independence. The result is a significantly underdeveloped and impoverished rural sector where basic public goods—notably physical infrastructure, law enforcement, judicial institutions, basic services, environmental protection, and regulatory frameworks—are almost entirely absent. The smallholding peasant economy is economically and technologically stagnant and environmentally unsustainable. In response, people are moving increasingly to the cities.

High rates of population growth and rapid urbanization, combined with economic stagnation, result in large numbers of increasingly educated youth entering an extremely restricted labor market. Unemployment and underemployment are pervasive among the young. A third of households in the capital have close relatives abroad (mostly in the United States or Canada). Their remittances allow a large group of people to avoid taking the lowest paid work in trade or other sectors, or to become self-employed, but instead to remain idle and near the poverty line. This pool of unemployed and disaffected youth totals several hundred thousands in the capital alone, while some 75,000 new migrants continue to enter the metropolitan area every year. Data show that metropolitan residents, although they have higher material living conditions than those in rural areas, live in fear of crime and violence. In conjunction with state fragility and political tensions, these circumstances create an explosive social situation unmitigated by the institutions responsible for providing security and rule of law.

Education is Key to Reducing Poverty and Inequality, but Access and Quality are Poor

Educational attainment in Haiti has increased over the last century, more so in urban than rural areas, but the quality of education remains alarmingly low. There are substantial differences in school attendance across regions, such that children and youths in the poorest regions fall behind their peers in richer areas. Moreover, the children of poor households have less education than children from nonpoor households.

For most Haitians, education is the key strategy for alleviating poverty; it is also associated with the reduction of inequalities. But access to education varies significantly in Haiti, as does its quality. Where poverty and inequality are risk factors for both crime and conflict, improvements in educational achievement not only increases human capital but can also indirectly mitigate these risks. Increasing investments in education will be crucial to reducing poverty and inequality, as well as mitigating crime and conflict over the longer term.

The Non-State Sector Provides Many Basic Services and Social Indicators are Improving

Social indicators such as literacy, life expectancy, infant mortality, and child malnutrition show that poverty is extensive in Haiti. About 40 percent of people cannot read and write; some 20 percent of children suffer from malnutrition; nearly half the population has no access to healthcare; and more than four-fifths have no clean drinking water. These indicators, however, also show that poverty in non-income terms has declined in recent decades.

State provision of infrastructure and basic services is limited outside Port-au-Prince and other urban centers. In response, private providers have made the difference between no education and some kind of schooling for large parts of the population. The same is true of health and other services. In rural areas especially, the non-state sector has provided a crucial safety net by offering access to services to a population mostly unserved by the state.

Among both private and public providers, the general quality of health and education services varies substantially and the costs of these essential services still restricts access by substantial numbers of the poor. Given the state's limited resources and capacity to provide services directly, development efforts should focus on improving the policy guidelines, coordination mechanisms, and regulatory frameworks for public-private partnerships.

Economic Growth is Needed but is Unlikely to Alleviate Poverty or Mitigate Conflict in the Short-term

Over the medium to long term, broad-based growth is needed to alleviate the high levels of poverty in Haiti. Economic growth is also crucial to reducing the unemployment that contributes to crime and violence in urban areas. Simulations of uniform growth in all sectors, however, reveal that the immediate impact of modest and even strong annual growth rates on poverty reduction will be relatively small. Hence growth alone will not alleviate poverty or mitigate conflict, particularly in the short run. Targeted interventions are thus needed to reduce poverty, attenuate violence and protect vulnerable groups. Strategic interventions to reduce poverty should aim to strengthen the key assets of the poor and should set regional priorities by taking account of geographic variations in poverty.

Core State Institutions Struggle to Provide Basic Conditions for Security and Development

The Haitian state continues to struggle to provide its citizens with minimum public goods. With only a limited capacity to establish security, provide basic infrastructure, and supply services, the state has been unable to create enabling conditions for economic growth and poverty reduction, or to prevent growing social tensions from challenging stability.

Significant financial constraints limit the state's capacity to be a driver of development and to respond to social risks. Haiti's GDP is extremely low and has been declining since 1980. In 2005, central government revenues were only 9 percent of GDP. The public sector has been further weakened by the volatility of aid flows—a result of political crises, corruption, and insecurity—and the channeling of assistance through the private sector and NGOs.

The Haitian state is also limited in its territorial reach, such that a large part of the rural population has practically no access to any public services. Constitutional provisions on political-administrative decentralization have not been implemented. As a result there is limited local participation in policy-making and deficient communication between the local and central levels for development planning.

Efforts to establish Haiti's first civilian police force as part of the international community's peacebuilding efforts in the 1990s were initially deemed largely successful. However, increased politicization and the weakness of accountability mechanisms within the HNP created a climate in which corruption and police links to criminal networks and drug trafficking could be exploited in later years. The judiciary is similarly weakened by corruption and political interference, circumstances that have undermined its independence. Strengthening the police and judiciary are not only crucial to ensuring security and justice; they are also necessary for the creation of an enabling environment for investments, economic growth, and development.

Improving the state's capacity to establish security and the rule of law, as well as to provide basic infrastructure and services, will be essential for mitigating conflict and enabling development. This will require a long-term commitment by national authorities and international partners. Before embarking on large-scale institutional capacity building programs, the government and donors should establish mechanisms to obviate the recurrence of practices that have undermined previous reform efforts.

Unconsolidated Democratic Institutions and "Entrepreneurs of Violence" have Undermined Political Leadership

Fourteen years of democratic transition in Haiti have not led to stable governance. Within a year of the 1990 elections, democracy was brutally repressed by the army and its supporters, using armed paramilitary groups that have been a feature of Haitian politics since Duvalier's *macoutes*. From President Aristide's return in 1994, democratic consolidation was undermined by deep conflicts among former democratic allies. The result was a political stalemate that lasted until his departure in 2004 and that undermined economic growth and state building. Moreover, the stalemate transformed important parts of the democratic movement—elements within the urban popular organizations—into violent government enforcers and criminal gangs that struggled for control of territory and state favors. Their area of operation and influence is in the urban slums and "popular areas," which provide an abundant pool of potential recruits.

Haiti's volatile political situation has been particularly dangerous because of the proliferation of armed groups with links to political organizations. The armed uprising of 2004 exacerbated trends that have been evident since the late 1990s, including the gradual disintegration of the Haitian police force, the prevalence of guns throughout the country, the absence of judicial institutions, and the violent activities of politically affiliated gangs. Given the return of former Haitian military officers (some credibly accused of severe human rights abuses), the breakdown of the penal system and the release of many prisoners, and the apparent impunity from sanctions for violence, armed elements continue to be a powerful force for destabilization. Any efforts to restore security will require a sustained international peacekeeping presence, the disarmament of militant groups, and the reconstitution of a national police force.

Yet Outside "Violent Urban Hotspots," Haiti has Remained Relatively Peaceful and has a Tradition of Strong Social Cohesion

Especially in fragile states, the ability of communities and households to work and live together by establishing bonds of mutual trust, as well as to penalize wrongdoing, are essential to maintaining people's livelihoods, security, and welfare. Social capital indicators suggest that robust cohesion at the community level has been crucial in preventing Haiti's institutional-political crisis from deteriorating into widespread social collapse or civil war. But there are wide urban-rural differences, and people in rural areas feel much safer in their daily lives than city dwellers. As the population shifts from rural to urban areas, the robust social cohesion that has characterized rural areas becomes less effective in mitigating social dislocation.

Restoring State Capacities and Reducing Urban Violence are Crucial to Breaking Haiti's Conflict-Poverty Trap

Haiti's deep and widespread poverty stems from a long history of failure to establish even the most basic enabling conditions for broad-based social and economic development. The state has struggled to provide basic services to the population and been dominated by a small elite that has made limited investments in infrastructure and services. Development, poverty reduction and conflict prevention will not be possible unless attention is paid to strengthening the state's capacity to provide basic public goods, including security and the rule of law. This is especially crucial in view of Haiti's very limited central government revenue base, which gives the state little leeway even in comparison to the average among low-income countries. Its financial and managerial resources must be used with an exceptionally strong sense of priorities.

A reduction in violence and an improvement in security conditions are of paramount importance in fostering sustainable development in Haiti. Very poor urban neighborhoods are explosive points of conflict in Haiti's development crisis, combining demographic, socioeconomic, institutional, and political risk factors. Violence and insecurity in the Port-au-Prince slums in particular has undermined the political process, fuelled conflict, and negatively affected development and reconstruction efforts. Joint multisectoral interventions in key urban areas (including Cité Soleil) that combine security and poverty reduction objectives will be essential for creating the conditions necessary for broad-based national development strategies.

The most important means of achieve a turnaround in Haiti is one that cannot be provided by donors but only by Haitians themselves: good leadership. Donors can support good leadership, supporting the "demand" for good governance, and by establishing incentives that reward good governance and penalize the opposite. Because of the centrality of corruption in undermining good leadership, transparency in public finances should be a foundation for the Bank and other donors' assistance to the newly elected Haitian government.

Haiti's development crisis is so multifaceted and the country's needs are so many that prioritizing reconstruction efforts and development assistance has proven difficult. This report argues that the focus should be on the restoration of core state functions—the provision of the public goods of security and the rule of law, infrastructure and basic services. Among the triangle of risk factors in the poverty-conflict trap, institutional capacity-building is a key entry point for breaking the cycle; improving demographic and socioeconomic outcomes and supporting political dialogue remain longer-term objectives. Institutional reform itself, however, requires a long-term engagement. Donors and the Haitian government should build on the existing International Cooperation Framework by prioritizing resources and monitoring progress, such that both donors and government can be held accountable for results.

Appendixes

Country at a Glance

Haiti at a Glance

Poverty and Social	Haiti	Latin America & Carib.	Low-Income
2004			
Population, mid-year *(millions)*	8.6	541	2,338
GNI per capita *(Atlas method, US$)*	390	3,600	510
GNI *(Atlas method, US$ billions)*	3.4	1,948	1,184
Average annual growth, 1998–04			
Population (%)	1.9	1.4	1.8
Labor force (%)	2.3	0.9	2.1
Most recent estimate (latest year available, 1998–04)			
Poverty *(% of population below national poverty line)*	—	—	—
Urban population *(% of total population)*	38	77	31
Life expectancy at birth *(years)*	52	71	58
Infant mortality *(per 1,000 live births)*	76	28	79
Child malnutrition *(% of children under 5)*	17	—	44
Access to an improved water source *(% of population)*	71	89	75
Literacy *(% of population age 15+)*	52	89	61
Gross primary enrollment *(% of school-age population)*	—	123	94
Male	—	126	101
Female	—	122	88

Development diamond*

Life expectancy

GNI per capita — Gross primary enrollment

Access to improved water source

—— Haiti   —— Low-income group

(*Continued*)

Haiti at a Glance (*Continued*)

KEY ECONOMIC RATIOS and LONG-TERM TRENDS

	1984	1994	2003	2004
GDP (US$ billions)	1.8	2.4	2.9	3.5
Gross capital formation/GDP	15.9	9.1	31.0	23.3
Exports of goods and services/GDP	17.5	5.4	16.4	14.2
Gross domestic savings/GDP	6.8	2.9	0.2	−3.7
Gross national savings/GDP	—	5.1	27.4	20.3
Current account balance/GDP	—	−4.0	−4.8	−2.8
Interest payments/GDP	0.4	0.0	0.5	1.0
Total debt/GDP	38.4	26.0	34.1	28.0
Total debt service/exports	—	2.7	4.1	7.7
Present value of debt/GDP	—	—	32.6	—
Present value of debt/exports	—	—	76.5	—

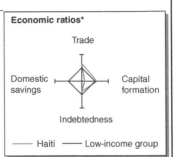

Economic ratios*

	1984–94	1994–04	2003	2004	2004–08
(average annual growth)					
GDP	−1.5	0.9	0.4	−3.8	3.1
GDP per capita	−3.4	−1.2	−1.4	−5.5	1.5
Exports of goods and services	−6.5	9.8	35.6	5.7	3.7

STRUCTURE of the ECONOMY

	1984	1994	2003	2004
(% of GDP)				
Agriculture	—	34.7	27.9	26.9
Industry	—	22.5	17.0	15.9
Manufacturing	—	13.7	8.4	7.0
Services	—	42.9	55.1	57.1
Household final consumption expenditure	82.3	87.5	91.3	98.3
General gov't final consumption expenditure	10.9	9.6	8.4	5.4
Imports of goods and services	26.5	11.7	47.2	41.2

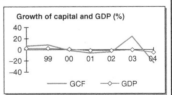

Growth of capital and GDP (%)

	1984–94	1994–04	2003	2004
(average annual growth)				
Agriculture	0.4	1.2	0.3	−4.4
Industry	−4.9	−7.2	1.0	−6.0
Manufacturing	−2.6	−7.4	0.5	−9.3
Services	0.7	4.4	0.4	11.5

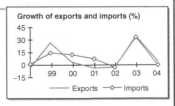

Growth of exports and imports (%)

(*Continued*)

Haiti at a Glance (*Continued*)

	1984–94	1994–04	2003	2004
Household final consumption expenditure	2.8	—	—	—
General gov't final consumption expenditure	−8.8	—	—	—
Gross capital formation	−9.0	6.5	24.9	−21.4
Imports of goods and services	−2.9	11.5	33.4	1.0

Note: 2004 data are preliminary estimates.

*The diamonds show four key indicators in the country (in bold) compared with its income-group average. If data are missing, the diamond will be incomplete.

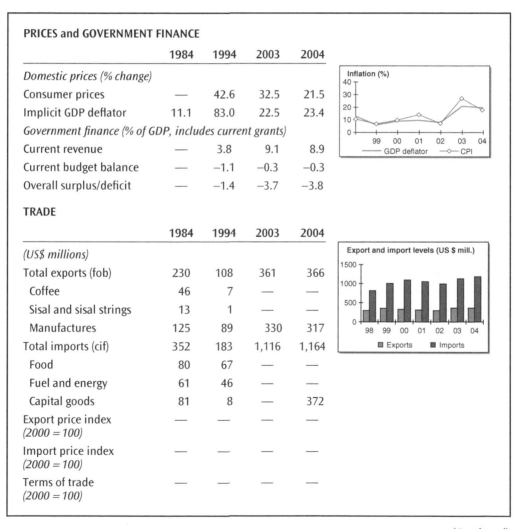

PRICES and GOVERNMENT FINANCE

	1984	1994	2003	2004
Domestic prices (% change)				
Consumer prices	—	42.6	32.5	21.5
Implicit GDP deflator	11.1	83.0	22.5	23.4
Government finance (% of GDP, includes current grants)				
Current revenue	—	3.8	9.1	8.9
Current budget balance	—	−1.1	−0.3	−0.3
Overall surplus/deficit	—	−1.4	−3.7	−3.8

TRADE

	1984	1994	2003	2004
(US$ millions)				
Total exports (fob)	230	108	361	366
Coffee	46	7	—	—
Sisal and sisal strings	13	1	—	—
Manufactures	125	89	330	317
Total imports (cif)	352	183	1,116	1,164
Food	80	67	—	—
Fuel and energy	61	46	—	—
Capital goods	81	8	—	372
Export price index (2000 = 100)	—	—	—	—
Import price index (2000 = 100)	—	—	—	—
Terms of trade (2000 = 100)	—	—	—	—

(*Continued*)

BALANCE of PAYMENTS

	1984	1994	2003	2004
(US$ millions)				
Exports of goods and services	—	131	461	502
Imports of goods and services	—	281	1,400	1,456
Resource balance	—	−150	−939	−953
Net income	—	2	−12	−13
Net current transfers	—	52	811	863
Current account balance	—	−97	−140	−98
Financing items (net)	—	142	130	156
Changes in net reserves	—	−45	10	−59
Memo:				
Reserves including gold (US$ millions)	23	41	207	213
Conversion rate (DEC, local/US$)	5.0	14.7	40.5	39.7

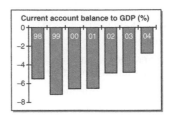

EXTERNAL DEBT and RESOURCE FLOWS

	1984	1994	2003	2004
(US$ millions)				
Total debt outstanding and disbursed	698	631	994	990
IBRD	0	0	0	0
IDA	150	248	212	194
Total debt service	34	4	51	106
IBRD	0	0	0	0
IDA	1	0	0	33
Composition of net resource flows				
Official grants	44	598	95	—
Official creditors	52	−3	15	−56
Private creditors	−5	0	0	0
Foreign direct investment (net inflows)	5	0	8	—
Portfolio equity (net inflows)	0	0	0	—
World Bank program				
Commitments	0	0	0	0
Disbursements	30	0	0	0
Principal repayments	0	0	0	27
Net flows	30	0	0	−27
Interest payments	1	0	0	6
Net transfers	29	0	0	−33

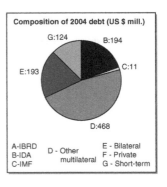

The World Bank Group: This table was prepared by country unit staff; figures may differ from other World Bank published data.

Demography

Table B.1. Population Size and Growth and Household Size in Urban and Rural Haiti, 1982–2003

Region	Urban			Rural			Total			
	Population	Avg. Household Size	Male to Female Ratio (%)	Population	Avg. Household Size	Male to Female Ratio (%)	Population	Avg. Household Size	Annual Population Growth 1982–2003 (%)	Pop. Density 2003 (pop/km²)
Artibonite	278,290	4.58	85.6	792,107	4.21	96.0	1,070,397	4.30	1.9	215
Center	90,843	4.65	90.7	474,200	4.51	100.8	565,043	4.53	2.2	154
Grand-Anse	90,095	4.47	93.2	513,799	4.45	105.7	603,894	4.46	1.0	182
North	295,624	5.20	85.1	477,922	5.07	96.9	773,546	5.12	1.6	367
Northeast	112,782	4.76	88.5	187,711	5.13	99.6	300,493	4.99	2.3	166
Northwest	102,338	5.30	84.9	342,742	5.00	96.0	445,080	5.07	2.1	205
West	2,070,799	4.72	86.5	1,022,900	4.39	95.9	3,093,699	4.61	3.4	641
South	98,506	4.96	89.3	528,805	4.80	105.3	627,311	4.82	1.1	225
Southeast	65,688	4.51	88.3	383,897	4.40	93.9	449,585	4.42	1.0	222
Haiti	3,204,965	4.76	86.7	4,724,083	4.55	98.5	7,929,048	4.63	2.2	286

Source: IHSI 2003.

Table B.2. Degree of Urbanization in Haiti and its Regions, 1982 and 2003 (percent)

Region	1982	2003
Artibonite	15.6	26.0
Center	10.7	16.1
Grand-Anse	10.6	14.9
North	21.1	38.2
Northeast	18.2	37.5
Northwest	11.3	23.0
West	49.1	66.9
South	11.7	15.7
Southeast	7.2	14.6
Haiti (entire country)	24.5	40.4

Source: IHSI 2003.

Table B.3. Average Household Size by Income Group and Place of Residence, 2001

	Region									Location			Total Haiti
	Artibonite	Center	Grand-Anse	North	North-east	North-west	West	South	South-east	Metro-politan	Urban	Rural	
Indigent													
	5.0	5.2	5.2	5.4	5.2	4.9	4.9	5.1	5.2	4.8	5.3	5.2	5.1
	(2.4)	(2.4)	(2.5)	(2.6)	(2.7)	(2.3)	(2.4)	(2.6)	(2.6)	(2.1)	(2.6)	(2.5)	(2.5)
Poor													
	4.8	4.9	5.0	5.2	5.1	4.8	4.7	4.9	4.9	4.9	5.1	4.9	4.9
	(2.4)	(2.4)	(2.5)	(2.6)	(2.7)	(2.3)	(2.3)	(2.5)	(2.6)	(2.2)	(2.6)	(2.5)	(2.5)
Nonpoor													
	2.6	3.5	3.4	4.2	3.8	3.1	3.9	3.8	3.2	4.2	3.6	3.3	3.6
	(2.0)	(2.2)	(2.1)	(2.7)	(2.1)	(1.8)	(2.8)	(2.3)	(2.0)	(2.5)	(2.4)	(2.1)	(2.3)
Total													
	4.4	4.7	4.7	5.0	5.0	4.6	4.4	4.7	4.5	4.5	4.7	4.6	4.6
	(2.5)	(2.4)	(2.5)	(2.7)	(2.7)	(2.3)	(2.4)	(2.5)	(2.6)	(2.4)	(2.6)	(2.5)	(2.5)

Note: Standard deviations in parentheses.
Source: Authors' calculations based on HLCS 2001.

Table B.4. Average Number of Household Members Aged Less than 15 Years, 2001

	Region									Area			
	Artibonite	Center	Grand-Anse	North	North-east	North-west	West	South	South-east	Metro-politan	Urban	Rural	Total Haiti
Indigent													
	2.1	2.5	2.3	2.3	2.4	2.1	1.9	2.2	2.6	1.7	2.3	2.2	2.2
	(1.8)	(1.9)	(1.9)	(1.9)	(1.9)	(1.8)	(1.7)	(1.9)	(1.9)	(1.5)	(1.9)	(1.9)	(1.9)
Poor													
	2.0	2.3	2.2	2.1	2.3	2.0	1.7	2.1	2.3	1.9	2.1	2.1	2.0
	(1.7)	(1.9)	(1.9)	(1.9)	(1.9)	(1.8)	(1.6)	(1.8)	(1.9)	(1.8)	(1.8)	(1.8)	(1.8)
Nonpoor													
	0.6	1.1	1.1	1.3	1.5	0.9	1.0	1.4	1.0	1.2	1.1	0.9	1.0
	(1.1)	(1.4)	(1.4)	(1.6)	(1.6)	(1.2)	(1.4)	(1.6)	(1.3)	(1.4)	(1.4)	(1.3)	(1.4)
Total													
	1.7	2.1	2.0	2.0	2.3	1.8	1.4	1.9	2.0	1.4	1.9	1.9	1.8
	(1.7)	(1.9)	(1.9)	(1.9)	(1.9)	(1.7)	(1.6)	(1.8)	(1.8)	(1.5)	(1.8)	(1.8)	(1.8)

Note: Standard deviations in parentheses.
Source: Authors' calculations based on HLCS 2001.

Data and Methodology

This section presents data sources and the methodologies used in the report to analyze poverty and labor markets in Haiti.

Data

Haiti is completing the first comprehensive household survey that covers both rural and urban areas. National household data are critical for making informed decisions on alleviating urban and rural poverty in Haiti. The analyses in this paper are based on the national households survey (l'Enquête sur les Conditions de Vie Haïti–the Haiti Living Conditions Survey [HLCS]) from 2001 (still unreleased). Population data are from publications produced by the statistical office (Institut Haitien de Statistique et d'Informatique–IHSI). The survey was undertaken in all nine regions (departments) and is representative at the regional level in Haiti. The dataset includes 7,186 households. It is the first time in Haiti's history that a survey of this magnitude has been conducted (see FAFO for more information).[118]

The household survey consists of 15 SPSS files (these files are dated 10.06.2004 and named Base de Données Mar). The Bank obtained them directly from the Haitian statistical agency through FAFO, the Norwegian institution that has worked with the statistical office. We have discovered a number of serious flaws. The most important flaw relates to the variable describing the metropolitan-urban-rural status of a household/individual, which is different in the various files. After discussions with the IHSI the only reliable data for metropolitan, urban, and rural levels are those based on the file with household information. Therefore, this data is used throughout the paper.

---

118. FAFO's website: www.fafo.no.

To calculate poverty, income including self-consumption has been used. Income is for the past 12 months based on a number of individual income sources and self-consumption is estimated value of consumption (and barter) of household production of crops, meat, and fish during the last week. First, respondents answer questions on consumption of own production and its market value. Second, an average unit price of each type of good was calculated for the entire sample, multiplied by the quantity consumed last week and multiplied by 52 weeks.

Poverty Methodology

The income-poverty measures are designed to count the poor and to diagnose the extent and distribution of poverty. The income-poverty measures proposed by Foster et al. (1984) are used throughout the paper. These are the headcount rate (P0), poverty gap (P1), and squared poverty gap (P2) measures. The former measures the magnitude of poverty and the latter two poverty measures assess both poverty magnitude and intensity.

The headcount rate is defined as the proportion of household heads (not the entire population) below the poverty line. One concern about applying the P0 measure is that each individual below the poverty line is weighted equally and, therefore, the principle of transfers is violated. A limitation of the measure is illustrated by the fact that it would be possible to reduce the P0 measure of poverty by transferring money from the very poor to lift some *richer* poor out of poverty, thereby increasing social welfare according to the measure. P0 takes no account of the degree of poverty and it is unaltered by policies that lead to the poor becoming even poorer.

One measure of poverty that takes this latter point into account (at least in weak form) is the poverty gap measure (P1). P1 is the product of incidence and average distance between the incomes of the poor and the poverty line. It can be interpreted as a per capita measure of the total economic shortfall relative to population. P1 distinguishes the poor from the not so poor and corresponds to the average distance to the poverty line of the poor. One problem with the poverty gap as an indicator of welfare is that poverty will increase by transfers of money from extreme poor to less poor (who become nonpoor), and from poor to nonpoor. Furthermore, transfers among the poor have no effect on the poverty gap measure.

The P2 measure of poverty is sensitive to the distribution among the poor as more weight is given to the poorest below the poverty line. P2 corresponds to the squared distance of income of the poor to the poverty line. Thus, moving from P0 toward P2 gives more weight to the poorest in the population.

This paper sets its poverty bar very low. To define "extreme poverty" it uses a US$1 a day poverty line, which is 2,681 gourdes per year.[119] Those who earn a per capita income above US$1 are above the extreme poverty line and therefore not extremely poor. The poverty lines used for rural, urban, and metropolitan areas are identical, as consumer price index data do not exist for different regions or locations in Haiti. This may slightly overestimate poverty in rural areas.

---

119. The conversion is based on the 2000 PPP. The questionnaire asks for information about income in the last 12 months and self-consumption in the last week (which is multiplied by 52 to obtain the annual self-consumption).

Labor Income Methodology–Quantile Regressions

Model: The underlying economic model used in the analysis will simply follow Mincer's (1974) human capital earnings function extended to control for a number of other variables that relate to location. In particular, we apply a semi-logarithmic framework that has the form:

$$\ln y_i = \varphi(x_i, z_i) + u_i \tag{1}$$

where $\ln y_i$ is the log of earnings or wages for an individual, i; x_i is a measure of a number of personal characteristics including human capital variables, etc.; and z_i represents location-specific variables. The functional form is left unspecified in equation (1). The empirical work makes extensive use of dummy variables in order to catch nonlinearities in returns to years of schooling, tenure, and other quantitative variables. The last component, u_i, is a random disturbance term that captures unobserved characteristics.

Quantile Regressions

Labor market studies usually make use of conditional mean regression estimators, such as OLS. This technique is subject to criticism because of several usually heroic assumptions underlying the approach. One is the assumption of homoskedasticity in the distribution of error terms. If the sample is not completely homogenous, this approach, by forcing the parameters to be the same across the entire distribution of individuals, may be too restrictive and may hide important information.

The method applied in this paper is that of quantile regressions. The idea is that one can choose any quantile and thus obtain many different parameter estimates on the same variable. In this manner, the entire conditional distribution can be explored. By testing whether coefficients for a given variable across different quantiles are significantly different, one implicitly also tests for conditional heteroskedasticity across the wage distribution. This is particularly interesting for developing countries such as Haiti where wage disparities are great and returns to, for example, human capital may vary across the distribution.

The method has many other virtues apart from being robust to heteroskedasticity. When the error term is nonnormal, for instance, quantile regression estimators may be more efficient than least squares estimators. Furthermore, since the quantile regression objective function is a weighted sum of absolute deviations, one obtains a robust measure of location in the distribution, and as a consequence the estimated coefficient vector is not sensitive to outlier observations on the dependent variable.[120]

The main advantage of quantile regressions is the semiparametric nature of the approach, which relaxes the restrictions on the parameters to be fixed across the entire distribution. Intuitively, quantile regression estimates convey information on wage differentials

---

120. That is, if $y_i - x_i'\hat{\beta}_\theta > 0$ then y_i can be increasing toward $+\infty$, or if $y_i - x_i'\hat{\beta}_\theta > 0$, y_i can be decreasing toward $-\infty$, without altering the solution $\hat{\beta}_\theta$. In other words, it is not the *magnitude* of the dependent variable that matters, but on which *side* of the estimated hyper plane the observation is. This is most easily seen by considering the first-order-condition, which can be shown to be given as (see Buchinsky 1998) $\frac{1}{n} \sum_{i=1}^{n} (\theta - \frac{1}{2} + \frac{1}{2}\mathrm{sgn}(y_i - x_i'\hat{\beta}_\theta)) x_i = 0$.

This can be seen both as a strength and weakness of the method. To the extent that a given outlier represents a feature of the "true" distribution of the population, one would prefer the estimator to be sensitive, at least to a certain degree, to such an outlier.

arising from nonobservable characteristics among individuals otherwise observationally equivalent. In other words, by using quantile regressions, we can determine if individuals who rank in different positions in the conditional distribution (i.e., individuals who have higher or lower wages than predicted by observable characteristics) receive different premiums to education, tenure, or to other relevant observable variables.

Formally, the method, first developed by Koenker and Basset (1978), can be formulated as

$$y_i = x_i' \beta_\theta + u_{\theta i} = \text{Quant}_\theta(y_i \mid x_i) = x_i' \beta_\theta \tag{2}$$

where $\text{Quant}_\theta(y_i \mid x_i)$ denotes the θth conditional quantile of y given x, and i denotes an index over all individuals, $i = 1, \ldots, n$.

In general, the θth sample quantile $(0 < \theta < 1)$ of y solves

$$\min_\beta = \frac{1}{n} \left\{ \sum_{i: y_i \geq x_i' \beta} \theta |y_i - x_i' \beta| + \sum_{i: y_i < x_i' \beta} (1 - \theta) |y_i - x_i' \beta| \right\}. \tag{3}$$

Buchinsky (1998) examines various estimators for the asymptotic covariance matrix and concludes that the design matrix bootstrap performs the best. In this paper, the standard errors are obtained by bootstrapping using 200 repetitions. This is in line with the literature.

Incidence of Education Level and Poverty Correlates

Education is also unequally distributed. International research shows that this can more easily be reduced than income inequality. However, research also shows that a reduction in education inequality affects the income distribution very little in the short run (Ferreira and others 2005).

Table D.1. Incidence of Education Level in Rural Haiti (percent), 2001

Quintile	No Education	Primary	Secondary	Tertiary
1 (poorest)	78.8	18.0	3.2	0.0
2	77.0	18.7	4.2	0.1
3	72.1	22.8	5.1	0.0
4	67.2	22.9	9.8	0.1
5 (richest)	56.6	26.6	16.6	1.2

Source: Authors' calculations based on HLCS 2001.

Table D.2. Incidence of Education Level in Urban Haiti (percent), 2001

Quintile	No Education	Primary	Secondary	Tertiary
1 (poorest)	65.2	26.3	8.2	0.4
2	58.3	27.4	13.9	0.4
3	61.6	26.4	12.0	0.0
4	50.8	31.7	17.2	0.3
5 (richest)	33.3	31.5	31.7	3.6

Source: Calculations based on HLCS 2001.

Table D.3. Incidence of Education Level in Metropolitan Haiti (percent), 2001

Quintile	No Education	Primary	Secondary	Tertiary
1 (poorest)	33.3	30.7	35.5	0.5
2	24.7	32.2	40.8	2.3
3	20.8	40.1	36.6	2.5
4	18.8	34.6	42.7	4.3
5 (richest)	10.0	19.5	52.4	18.2

Source: Calculations based on HLCS 2001.

Table D.4. Analysis of Poverty Correlates in Haiti, 2001

P0	dF/dx	t-stat	Variables in column 1 interacted w. rural (R*)	dF/dx	t-stat
Age	−0.00	−2.34	R*Age	0.00	0.57
Female*	−0.03	−1.23	R*Female*	0.08	2.22
Family size	0.12	7.73	R*Family size	−0.01	−0.57
Squared			R*Squared		
family size	−0.01	−6.02	family size	0.00	1.61
Primary education*	−0.20	−6.64	R*Primary education*	0.06	1.66
Secondary education*	−0.27	−7.85	R*Secondary Education*	−0.02	−0.48
Tertiary education*	−0.43	−5.42	R*Tertiary education*	−0.13	−0.51
Migrated*	−0.08	−2.36	R*Migrant*	0.04	0.88
Work tenure >5 years*	−0.10	−1.64	R*Work tenure >5 years*	0.04	0.42
No info (work ten.)*	−0.05	−0.75	R*no info (work ten.)*	−0.03	−0.41
Industry*	0.18	2.35	R*Industry*	0.02	0.22
Agriculture*	0.16	2.36	R*Agriculture*	0.08	0.84
Service*	0.18	2.82	R*Service*	0.03	0.31
Inactive*	0.24	3.58	R*Inactive*	0.12	1.27
Catholic*	0.03	0.33	R*Catholic*	0.02	0.16
Baptist*	0.03	0.29	R*Baptist*	0.09	0.78
Other Religion*	0.02	0.23	R*Other Religion*	0.07	0.59
Social*	0.03	1.09	R*Social*	−0.12	−3.39
Rural*	−0.02	−0.13			
Southeast*	0.22	3.56	R*Southeast*	−0.09	−1.29
North*	0.25	6.08	R*North*	−0.04	−0.67
Northeast*	0.47	10.29	R*Northeast*	−0.18	−2.41
Artibonite*	0.38	9.42	R*Artibonite*	−0.25	−5.00
Center*	0.28	5.70	R*Center*	−0.15	−2.55
South*	0.20	3.97	R*South*	0.03	0.45
Grand-Anse*	0.34	7.24	R*Grand-Anse*	−0.21	−3.57
Northwest*	0.22	4.43	R*Northwest*	0.00	0.05

Note: Number of observations: 7,031; (*) dF/dx is for discrete change of dummy variable from 0 to 1; t is the test of the underlying coefficient being equal to 0.

Source: Authors' calculations based on HLCS 2001.

Poverty Profile

Literacy is strongly related to poverty. In other words, being able to read is important in determining the likelihood of being in poverty. In Haiti, the P0 is 34 percent for household heads who are literate, and 60 percent for those who are not. Not surprisingly, these headcounts are high compared to other countries in Latin America and the Caribbean. A large difference in poverty exists between household heads living in metropolitan and rural areas. P0 for heads who can read is 17 percent in the metropolitan area compared to 47 and 46 percent in rural and other urban areas, respectively. Language skills are also strongly related to poverty.

In Haiti, the P0 is lower when the head speaks French, i.e., 28 and 49 percent for the French speakers and non-French speakers, respectively.[121] The poverty headcount is much lower for French-speaking Haitians in urban areas (25 percent) than in rural areas (66 percent).[122]

Education levels are very strongly related to poverty. Household heads with completed tertiary education are much less likely to experience poverty than those who have completed secondary or primary education only. There appears to be a large difference in P0 between household heads with no education (61 percent) and household heads with completed primary education (43 percent). Household heads who have completed secondary education are much better off (25 percent are poor) than those with only primary education. Of the household heads with completed tertiary education, only 5 percent were

---

121. It is worth noting that very few heads of household in the sample speak French.

122. Some data limitations have been observed, such as: (1) only 39 households speak French at home; (2) 94 household heads have completed tertiary education; and (3) work tenure findings are based on only 1,588 observations.

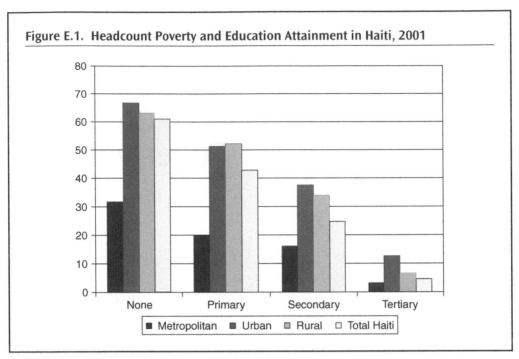

Figure E.1. Headcount Poverty and Education Attainment in Haiti, 2001

Source: Authors' calculations based on HLCS 2001.

extremely poor in 2001. These findings indicate that education is a very important key to poverty reduction in Haiti as elsewhere.

Figure 6.1 presents the location differences in P0 for the four education levels. The chart clearly shows that poverty at any given education level is much more widespread in rural areas than in the metropolitan areas. This is also the case for other urban areas that perform worse than rural areas; only household heads with primary education are less poor in urban than rural areas. For all levels P0 is only slightly higher in rural areas if it is higher at all. Obviously, the data presented do not take into consideration that the quality of education may be lower in rural areas.

Figure E.1 shows that there are very large differences in poverty levels by education attained. The difference has most likely increased over time as in other countries (no household data are available to address this further since the 2001 survey is the very first the country has undertaken). Table E.1 shows that of household members with an income that places them in the lowest two income quintiles, more than 50 percent have not completed any education level, and only around 30 percent have completed primary education.[123]

Elder household heads are more likely to experience poverty than younger household heads. In Haiti, only 40 percent of households headed by a member younger than age 25 are below the extreme poverty line. This compares to 52 percent for households headed by a member older than 65 years of age. The latter group has the lowest average income of any

123. Note that Table 6.2 includes 20,074 individuals.

Table E.1. Highest Education Level Completed (percent), 2001

	Quintile				
	1 (poorest)	2	3	4	5 (richest)
No education	53.2	50.7	46.1	38.9	21.1
Primary	33.4	32.0	32.3	34.1	29.3
Secondary	13.3	17.1	21.1	26.1	44.6
Tertiary	0.1	0.2	0.6	0.9	5.0

Note: Age 15 and above included. No. observations 20,074.
Source: Authors' calculations based on HLCS 2001.

age group, which may be explained in part by lack of old age pensions in Haiti. The P0 of the population groups aged 25 to 44 and 45 to 65 was 47 and 51 percent, respectively, in 2001. Thus, the older the heads of household, the more likely they are to be poor. Therefore, this does not reflect a life cycle profile of poverty, but it illustrates that many household heads are born poor (mainly due to inadequate assets); assets are only sparsely accumulated, and when household heads reach old age most assets are depleted. As there are very few social protection programs available for elderly people, there currently exist few mechanisms that can take households headed by an older person out of poverty. Other countries in the region such as Brazil have changed this pattern by introducing old age pensions for all poor elderly people. Finally, it is worth noting that for all age groups the likelihood of falling below the poverty line is more than double for urban and rural dwellers than it is for metropolitan dwellers.

Female-headed households are marginally more likely to be poor than male-headed households, with 50 and 48 percent of female- and male-headed households, respectively, likely to be poor in Haiti as a whole. However, in rural areas female-headed households (62 percent of which are poor) are much more likely to fall below the indigence poverty line than are male-headed households (54 percent are poor). However, these income poverty figures are only part of the myriad factors that affect a poor woman's well-being.

The HLCS data on domestic violence show that the most common forms of violence that women have experienced are forced sex and being pushed, kicked, or slapped. Women experienced slightly more of these forms of violence than men claimed to have committed. Of those women who were at any time beaten, around 50 percent were beaten roughly every month.

Migrants experience less poverty than nonmigrants do in Haiti as a whole. Heads who migrated from one region to another experienced 24 percentage points less poverty than did heads who never left; 30 percent of the former and 54 percent of the latter group fell below the US$1 per day poverty line, a difference of 80 percent. One explanation for this is that migrants are better endowed than nonmigrants (Justesen and Verner 2005, Egset 2004). For rural areas the difference is much smaller (12 percent) between *stayers* in rural areas in one region and *leavers* to rural areas in another region. Thus, there is little difference between rural dwellers who never migrated and those who did migrate to a region different from that of their birth.

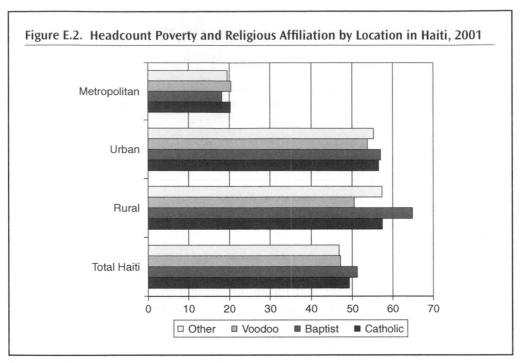

Figure E.2. Headcount Poverty and Religious Affiliation by Location in Haiti, 2001

Source: Authors' calculations based on HLCS 2001.

Religious belief has only marginal impact on poverty status. The three major religions by number of adherents in Haiti are Catholicism, Baptism, and Voodoo, and 49, 51, 47 percent are poor, respectively, for each religion. Household heads with social capital are less likely to fall into poverty in Haiti as a whole. This finding also holds true for heads in metropolitan areas, but even more so in rural areas. The relationships among extended family members and neighbors form an important informal social safety net for sharing assets, responsibilities, and risks. Household heads who are members of one or more organizations are less likely (51 percent are poor) to be poor than their peers who are nonmembers (60 percent are poor).

One explanation for this finding could be that members of organizations have more ties to other members and friends who can assist economically or emotionally in difficult situations.

Help from friends, perhaps related to political affiliation, may therefore replace safety nets, financial institutions, and credit to smooth economic cycles in the household. There are large differences across the nine regions in Haiti. The heads with social capital are far less likely to experience poverty in the Grand-Anse, North, South, Southeast, and West regions. There is very little difference in the Northwest and Center regions. In the Northeast and Antibonite regions household heads with social capital are more likely to experience poverty. This may be explained by large out-migrations from these regions.

The self-employed are more likely to experience poverty than employees. The incidence of poverty for the self-employed was 51 percent while that of employees was 21 percent in 2001. Work position data show that for all locations (metropolitan, rural, and urban),

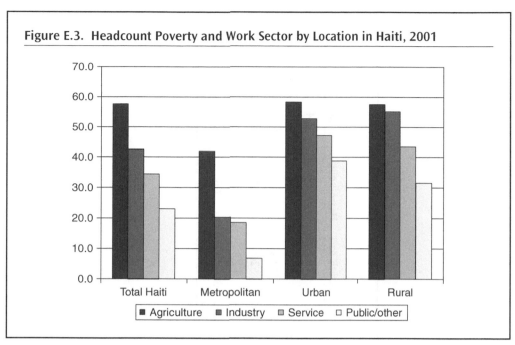

Figure E.3. Headcount Poverty and Work Sector by Location in Haiti, 2001

Source: Authors' calculations based on HLCS 2001.

household heads who are self-employed are more likely to experience poverty than employees are. In the metropolitan area the likelihood of falling below the poverty line is nearly four times higher for a self-employed person compared to an employee and in rural areas the likelihood is double.

Those who work in agriculture are far more likely to be poor than others. This suggests that productivity in agriculture is lower than in services or industry. The P0 is 58 percent in agriculture, but 43 percent among industrial workers, and 34 percent among service workers. Public sector workers experienced the lowest poverty incidence, 23 percent. The sectoral poverty pattern, highest in agriculture and lowest in public sector, is similar for metropolitan, urban, and rural areas although the poverty rates differ according to location (Figure E.3). The main explanation for the high poverty rate in agriculture can be traced to migration out of the sector and into higher wage services by some of the most skilled and, in part, to the structure of land ownership and the quality of land and climate. Rural land ownership is characterized by a large number of small farms with an insufficient area to sustain a family by agricultural employment alone.

Income poverty among landless rural dwellers is not necessarily higher than among households with land. P0 for landless households is 36.3 percent compared to 64.8 and 46.8 percent for landholdings of 0.5 or less hectare and 6–10 hectares, respectively. Only households with more than 10 hectares experience less income poverty than landless households; of the farms with more than 10 hectares of land, 31 percent were poor. It is worth emphasizing that only 1.8 percent of farms are larger than 10 hectares in Haiti (see Section 9). Moreover, extreme poverty is monotonically decreasing with farm size in Haiti (Table E.2).

Table E.2. Poverty Incidence by Farm Size (percent), 2001

	Arti-bonite	Center	Grand-Anse	North	North-east	North-west	West	South	South-east	Metro-politan	Urban	Rural	Haiti
No land	59.7	44.2	58.3	60.2	68.6	67.7	24.7	54.4	50.1	19.5	52.4	54.8	36.3
0–0.5 ha	64.9	70.4	75.9	70.1	96.5	68.5	39.9	73.0	56.8	38.6	63.7	65.4	64.8
0.5–2 ha	58.5	62.1	66.2	61.8	94.0	65.1	43.6	67.0	59.8	100.0	62.3	60.1	60.5
2–6 ha	48.7	44.9	49.4	55.4	78.3	64.9	48.4	42.6	52.9	NA	45.4	52.7	51.2
6-10 ha	48.1	33.9	40.0	47.2	55.5	59.5	41.2	53.1	62.2	NA	40.4	47.6	46.8
>10 ha	39.1	32.7	36.0	NA	NA	13.1	32.9	25.3	23.7	NA	42.0	28.8	30.6

Note: 7,177 households used and only 81 farms are larger than 10 ha. NA: not available.

Source: Authors' calculations based on HLCS 2001.

Table E.3. Probability of being Employed in the Nonagricultural Sector, 2001

	Nonagricultural Employment		Low-Productivity Nonagricultural Employment		High-Productivity Nonagricultural Employment	
	dF/dx	T	dF/dx	T	dF/dx	T
Female*	0.50	12.41	0.13	5.75	0.11	3.74
Family size	0.03	3.64	0.02	4.93	0.00	−0.71
Primary education*	0.17	3.97	−0.06	−2.46	0.21	5.70
Secondary education*	0.33	7.41	−0.07	−2.63	0.37	8.48
Tertiary education*	0.35	4.99	−0.14	−3.84	0.68	6.55
Migrated*	0.18	2.43	0.00	0.16	0.03	0.75
Social capital*	0.08	1.79	−0.01	−0.43	0.03	0.77
Land per capita (ha)	0.00	5.12	0.00	2.84	0.00	4.93
Rural*	−0.30	−2.95	−0.12	−2.19	−0.28	−3.83
R-female*	−0.05	−1.01	0.16	5.23	0.12	3.01
R-fam size*	−0.02	−2.11	0.00	−0.30	−0.01	−1.41
R-primary*	0.02	0.32	0.08	2.47	−0.01	−0.35
R-secondary*	0.04	0.58	0.10	2.06	0.08	1.41
R-migrant*	0.04	0.44	0.08	1.92	0.09	1.69
R-social capita*	−0.03	−0.61	−0.01	−0.49	0.06	1.37
R-ha per cap.	0.00	0.27	0.00	2.73	0.00	1.09
Southeast*	−0.61	−6.47	−0.07	−1.38	−0.21	−4.47
North*	−0.30	−3.10	0.19	4.18	−0.21	−5.25
Northeast*	−0.54	−5.44	0.23	3.93	−0.27	−6.43
Artibonite*	−0.49	−5.32	0.13	3.27	−0.29	−7.79
Center*	−0.58	−6.33	0.01	0.25	−0.29	−8.16
Southeast*	−0.49	−4.81	0.02	0.36	−0.22	−4.94
Grand-Anse*	−0.43	−4.26	0.16	3.31	−0.27	−6.84
Northwest*	−0.47	−4.69	0.01	0.29	−0.19	−3.92
R-Southeast*	0.32	4.76	0.09	1.12	0.15	1.93
R-North*	0.18	2.09	−0.03	−0.77	0.04	0.49
R-Northeast*	0.29	4.04	−0.05	−0.89	0.20	1.79
R-Artibonite*	0.23	2.79	−0.10	−2.72	0.19	2.79
R- Center*	0.27	3.68	−0.06	−1.24	0.36	4.55
R-South*	0.24	2.83	−0.03	−0.57	0.13	1.65
R-Grand-A.*	0.23	2.81	−0.10	−2.65	0.31	4.00
R-Northwest*	0.29	4.13	0.07	1.14	0.14	1.73
Pseudo R2	0.50		0.16		0.37	

Note: R-identifies the rural variable interacted with another variable Excluded variables: No education and West region. Number of obs = 4,349. (*) dF/dx is for discrete change of dummy variable from 0 to 1; t is the test of the underlying coefficient being equal to 0.

Source: Authors' calculations based on HLCS 2001.

The rural poor are primarily smallholders, sharecroppers, and informal wageworkers who depend on a diverse strategy of income generating activities in which the subsistence production of corn, millet, bananas and plantains, beans, yams, sweet potatoes, and small animals predominates. Any crop surplus is sold at the local market. Rice is grown in the areas of the country where irrigation systems have been introduced. In addition to subsistence production, Haiti's peasants have traditionally grown crops—principally sugar, coffee, cacao, indigo, sisal, and cotton—to sell for cash and at times to the export market. Small farmers lack modern production technology, basic infrastructure to store harvests to take advantage of cyclical price fluctuations, technical assistance to improve productivity, and organized marketing facilities. Family income is therefore highly variable and there is little opportunity for saving. Families have very few assets, including education, and are very vulnerable.

The analyses of participation in nonfarm activities are multivariate and estimate a probit model of involvement in nonfarm activities as a primary occupation on a range of individual, household, and geographical characteristics. The specification of the model draws on findings above, which suggest that the choice of primary occupation is affected by for example education and gender. Rather than reporting the parameter estimates, which are difficult to interpret on their own, the table presents the marginal effects associated with each explanatory variable. These can be interpreted as indicating the effect of a percentage change in the explanatory variable on the probability of involvement in nonfarm business activities, taking all other variables in the specification at their means. For dummy variables, the marginal effect is calculated as the change in the dependent variable associated with a move from a value of zero for the dummy, to one, holding all other variables constant at mean values. The nonfarm subsectors are designated as either high return or low return depending on the average annual earnings accruing to the individuals whose primary occupation is in that sector. If the average annual wage is below the extreme poverty line (appendix c), the sub-sector is designated as low return, or low productivity sector. Conversely, if the average annual return from a sub-sector is above the poverty line, the sub-sector is designated as high return.

Access to Basic Services in Haiti

Table F.1. Access to Basic Services

| | Carrefour Feuille | | Cité Soleil |
	Kay Alfred/Sicot Prolonge	Fort Mercredi	Boston
Access to water	■ Purchase in buckets ■ Collection of rain-water	■ Purchase in buckets at Gran Ravin or Route des Dalles ■ Access to water system provided by CAMEP (1) ■ Neighbors	■ Purchase at water point (3)
Price of a 5-liter container	■ 2 to 3 gourdes (CAMEP) ■ 5 to 7 gourdes (private reservoir)	■ 1 to 5 gourdes	■ 1 gourde/water point ■ 4 gourdes in period of scarcity
Electricity	Electricity line	Electricity line	Electricity line
Price for connection	50 gourdes/month	500 gourdes/month	NP
Sanitation	■ 6 out of 10 have a latrine, 3 in bad condition	■ 6 out of 10 have latrines ■ 2 latrines under construction ■ 1 toilet (WC)	■ 5 out of 10 have a latrine, 2 in bad condition ■ Disposal of excrement in neighborhood canals
Sharing of latrines	Yes	Yes	Yes
Education		■ Community school (2) ■ Religious school ■ Private school	
Health	No health care facilities	No health care facilities	Basic facilities and hospital

Table F.2. Typology of Non-State Basic Service Providers in Haiti

Types of non-state service provider	Domains	Coordination/collaboration mechanisms
Grassroots level community organizations:	Basic services in social protection and insurance, health and education. May support community schools in remote, poor areas. There are 1,944 community schools in Haiti, of which 312 receive subsidies from either the Ministry, PTAs, or NGOs/donors.	Fragile and very locally focused, rarely operating in a concerted fashion at the regional or national levels. Cooperatives, peasant associations (*gwoupman paysan*), and urban neighborhood groups (*gwoupman katye*).
Haitian NGOs:	Typically multisectoral, covering a range of activities (health, education, social protection, etc.) and sometimes targeting the neediest groups.	Provide services directly or support and train community groups to do this.
Religious groups and associations (Catholic, Protestant, and Voodoo):	Education sector (religious schools account for an estimated two-thirds of the sector. Catholic schools offer some of Haiti's best schools; mission schools (Baptist, Protestant, Adventist, and Pentecostal) receive significant foreign support; Presbyterian schools are generally poorer and vary more in quality.	Often ties to church groups in other countries.
Private sector for-profit	Across sectors, major quality variations, from elite private schools for the rich, to informal schools operating out of shacks for the poor. In health, private entrepreneurs range from elite private doctors to traditional "leaf doctors," voodoo doctors, missionaries, and a range of charlatans and ambulatory drug dispensers with no formal training.	6,000 of the 11,000+ private schools in Haiti belong to the *Bishops Conference of Catholic Schools*, the *Federation of Protestant Schools*, or the *Confederation of Independent Private Schools*. An umbrella organization, *Fondation Haitienne d'Enseignement Privé* (FONHEP), was founded in the late 1980s with support from USAID to coordinate quality enhancement. Some collaboration with the state, no public funding. Membership has recently declined, app. 3,500 schools.
International NGOs (Save the Children, CRS, Care, etc.)	Supporting local partners to implement programs as part of a more holistic social protection and development program across sectors.	Most international NGOs have cooperative agreements established with the government.
Bilateral and multilateral agencies (IDB, WB, USAID, UNDP, EU, etc.)	Across sectors, both through the state and non-state providers. Their funds are either directly delivered to international grantees (such as the INGOs listed above), or channeled through the state.	The Interim Cooperation Framework (2004) and the Sector Tables established by this framework provide coordination structure; practice varies.

World Bank (2005, 2006), Salmi (1998).

Table F.3. The Haitian Administrative Governance Structure

Level	Central State				Collectivités territoriales
	Executive	Legislative	Judiciary	Services (example)	
National	President Prime Minister Cabinet All operational levels	Senat (33) Chamber of Deputies (83) Parliament	Supreme Court Appeals Courts (5)	Ministry of Agriculture, Natural Resources and Rural Development (MARNDR)	N.B. Participation of one delegate from Conseil Interdépartemental in the Cabinet. Never put in place.
Department (10) Level of services decentralized from national ministries	Delegate Represents the executive and exercises state oversight over the CTs. The Transitional Government has nominated new Delegates.	3 Senators per Department	First Instance Courts (15)	Departmental Agriculture Agency (DDA) Has staff but often lacks capacity; corruption cases	Conseil InterDépartemental (CID)/Consultative body Conseil départemental Assemblée départementale None of these structures have been put into place
Arrondissement (40–41) – territorial subdivision under Vice Delegate	Vice Delegate Represents the Delegate and exercises oversight				
Municipality – *agglomeration of sections communales* (133–140) – *cadre d'action de certains services publics : police, collecte d'impôt, état-civil* – *cadre des services déconcentrés de certains ministères*			*Tribunal de Paix (approx. 200)* Not always operational, depending on municipality	*Bureau Agricole Communal (BAC)* *Regroupements de BAC par manque de ressources*	Municipal Council Relatively operational. Mayor appointed by Transitional Government in largest cities. Municipal Assembly (including representatives of sections communales) Mostly non-existent.
Quartier – Certain public services: police, justice			*Tribunal de Paix* Not always operational, depending on *quartier*		
Section communale – smallest administrative unit in Haïti (565)					Administrative Council of the Section Communale (CASEC) Elections in 1990, 1995, 2000. Structures rarely operational and often arbitrary. Assembly of Section Communale Never put in place.

Cohesion and Violence in Haiti

Table G.1. Confidence in Selected Institutions by Region

Confidence or Great Confidence in . . .	Metropolitan Area	Other Urban	Rural	All
Schools	94	97	94	95
Churches	91	96	94	94
Public health services	68	82	84	80
Police	55	70	71	67
Radio	54	63	63	61
NGOs	50	58	63	59
International org.	46	60	63	58
Civil service	37	62	60	55
Municipal adm.	23	45	54	45
Parliament	21	33	39	34
Popular org.	20	33	38	33
Political parties	14	19	21	19
Houngan, Voodoo	6	7	12	10
N	1268827	798959	3281743	5349529
Uwn	993	1159	4949	7101

Table G.2. Indicators of Fear of Crime by Region

	Metropolitan Area	Other Urban	Rural	All	Wn	Uwn
Feel safe or unsafe at home?						
Always save	8	45	49	39	2016530	3048
Most of the time safe	33	40	36	36	1857953	2448
Often unsafe	43	9	10	18	930851	1004
Most of the time unsafe	15	5	5	8	406405	440
Feel afraid to go to . . . Neighbors?						
Often or sometimes	25	21	19	21	1104445	1382
Never	67	74	76	74	3916095	5304
Not relevant	8	5	5	6	294741	363
People in this town or area?						
Often or sometimes	35	23	22	25	1328150	1667
Never	57	72	73	69	3664587	4974
Not relevant	9	5	5	6	326680	408
Local market?						
Often or sometimes	38	23	22	26	1388025	1710
Never	57	73	73	69	3698732	5036
Not relevant	5	4	5	4	235838	308
Nearest larger town?						
Often or sometimes	47	27	24	30	1579350	1923
Never	49	67	67	63	3316999	4559
Not relevant	5	6	9	7	393212	536
Port-au-Prince?						
Often or sometimes	54	31	24	32	1690005	2069
Never	43	52	45	45	2378538	3129
Not relevant	4	17	31	22	1172743	1742
Total	100	100	100	100	5241286	6940

References

Amnesty International. 2005. "Disarmament Delayed, Justice Denied." July 27. http://web. amnesty.org/library/Index/ENGAMR360382004?open&of=ENG-HTI.

Aristide, Marx V. and Laurie Richardson. 1994. "Haiti's popular resistance." In James Ridgeway, ed., *The Haiti Files–Decoding the Crisis.* Washington, D.C.: Essential Books/ Azul Editions.

Barro, Robert. 1991. "Economic Growth in a Cross-Section of Countries." *Quarterly Journal of Economics.*

Barthelemy, Gérard, Alejandro Alvarez, Alicia Carnaval, Myrtha Gilbert, Patrick Pierre-Louis, and Georges Proulx. 1999. "Justices en Haiti." UNDP. Processed.

Berdal, Mats, and David M. Malone, eds. 2000. *Greed and Grievance: Economic Agendas in Civil Wars.* Boulder, Colo.: Lynne Rienner Publishers.

Bized. "Government Expenditure Theories–Public Goods and Merit Goods–What are they and who gets them?" Institute for Fiscal Studies (IFS) Virtual Economy. http:// www.bized.ac.uk/virtual/economy.

Bourguignon, F., F. Ferreira, and N. Lustig. 2005. *The Microeconomics of Income Distribution Dynamics in East Asia and Latin America.* Washington, D.C.: The World Bank.

Buchinsky, M. 1998. "Recent Advances in Quantile Regression Models—A Practical Guideline for Empirical Research." *The Journal of Human Resources* 33(1):88–126.

Buvinic and Morrison. n.d.: "Violence in Latin America." Inter-American Development Bank, Washington, D.C.

CIDA (Canadian International Development Agency). 2004. "Canadian Cooperation with Haiti: Reflecting on a Decade of Difficult Partnership." http://www.oecd.org/dataoecd/ 41/45/34095943.pdf.

CCI Groupe Thématique: Securité et Gouvernance Politique. 2004. "Justice–Prisons–Droits Humains." Rapport du Sous-Groupe. http://haiticci.undg.org/uploads/ACFB20.doc.

Card, D. 1998. "The Causal Effect of Education on Earnings." In O. Ashenfelter and D. Card, eds., *Handbook of Labor Economics* Vol. 3.

Carey, Henry. 2003. "Country at the Crossroads: Country Profiles for Haiti." UN Online Network in Public Administration and Finance. http://unpan1.un.org/intradoc/groups/ public/documents/nispacee/unpan016030.pdf.

Center on International Cooperation and Political Economy Research Institute. 2005. "Public Finance and Post-Conflict Statebuilding. Meeting of Case Study Authors and Advisory Committee, Meeting Summary."

Collier, Paul. 1999a. "The Economic Consequences of Civil War." *Oxford Economic Papers* 51:168–83.

———. 1999b. "Doing Well Out of War." The World Bank, Washington, D.C.

———. 2000. "Policy for Post-conflict Societies: Reducing the Risk of Renewed Conflict." The Economics of Political Violence Conference, March 18–19, Princeton University.

Collier, Paul, and Anke Hoeffler. 2002. "Greed and Grievance in Civil War." WPS/2002-01. The World Bank, Washington, D.C.

Collier, Paul, V.L. Elliott, Håvard Hegre, Anke Hoeffler, Marta Reynal-Querol, and Nicholas Sambanis. 2003. *Breaking the Conflict Trap: Civil War and Development Policy.* Washington, D.C.: The World Bank.

Corten. 2000. "Diabolisation et mal politique : Haiti, misere et politique Montréal : Éditions du CIDIHCA."

Dailey, Peter. 2003. "Haiti: The Fall of the House of Aristide." *The New York Review of Books*, March 13.

Deibert, Michael. 2005. "Notes from the Last Testament: the Struggle for Haiti." New York: Seven Stories Press.

Demographics and Health Surveys (DHS). 2000. http://www.measuredhs.com.

Diederich, Bernard. 2005. "Un an après. Haïti : Retour sur la chute de l'idole." http://www.alterpresse.org.

Dobbins, James (Rand Corporation, former U.S. envoy to Haiti). 2005. Statement at the workshop on "Development, Security, and Statebuilding in Haiti." World Bank, November 15, 2005.

Dorsainvil, Daniel. 2005. "Rapport d'Evaluation de la Mise en Oeuvre du Cadre de Cooperation Interimaire." The World Bank, Washington, D.C. Processed.

Easterly and Gatti. 2000. "What Causes Political Violence? A Research Outline." Development Research Group, The World Bank.

EBCM. 2000. Enquête budget-consommation des ménages, 1999–2000.

Egset, W. 2004. "Rural Livelihoods." In *Haiti Living Conditions*, Volume II. Port au Prince: Institut Haitien de Statistique et d'Informatique.

Egset, W. and Mark Mattner. 2005. "Urban Violence in Haiti: Socio-economic, institutional, and political causes." Unpublished working paper, The World Bank, Washington, D.C.

Elbadawi, I.A.. 1999. "Civil Wars and Poverty: The Role of External Interventions, Political Rights and Economic Growth." The World Bank, Washington, D.C. Processed.

Eichler, R., P. Auxila, and J. Pollock. 2001. "Output-based Health Care: Paying for Performance in Haiti." Public Policy for the Private Sector Series, World Bank Private Sector and Infrastructure Network.

Fatton, Robert, Jr. 2002. "Haiti's Predatory Republic: The Unending Transition to Democracy." Boulder, Colo.: Lynne Rienner Publishers, Inc.

Ferreira, F., and P. Lanjouw. 2001. "Rural Poverty and Nonfarm Employment in Brazil." *World Development* 29(3):509–28.

Ferreira, F., and P. Leite. 2001. "Education Expansion and Income Distribution." Department of Economics, PUC-RIO.

Filmer, D., and L. Pritchett. 1997. "Attaining Millennium Development Goals in Health: Isn't Economic Growth Enough?" ADB. Processed.

Foster, Greer, and Thorbecke. 1984. "A class of decomposable poverty measures." *Econométrica* 52:761–65.

Fukuyama, Francis. 2004. *State-building: Governance and World Order in the 21st Century.* Ithaca, N.Y.: Cornell University Press.

Ghani Ashraf, Clare Lockhard, and Michael Carnahan. 2005. *Closing the Sovereignty Gap: An Approach to State-Building.* London: Overseas Development Institute, Working Paper 253.

Girault, Christian A. 1980. "Le café en Haïti." Bordeaux: Centre National de la Recherche Scientifique (CNRS).

Griffin, Thomas M. 2004. "Haiti. Human Rights Investigation: November 11–21, 2004." Center for the Study of Human Rights, University of Miami School of Law

Groupe d'Intervention de la Police Nationale d'Haiti, (GIPNH).

Heckman, James J., and B. Singer. 1984. "A Method for Minimizing the Impact of Distributional Assumptions in Econometric Models for Duration Data." *Econométrica* 52(2): 271–320.

Heinl, Robert D., Jr., and Nancy G. Heinl. 1978. *Written in Blood—The Story of the Haitian People 1492–1971*. Boston: Houghton Mifflin Company.

Human Rights Watch (HRW). 1993. "Silencing a People: The Destruction of Civil Society in Haiti." Washington, D.C.

———. 1996. "Haiti: Thirst For Justice. A Decade of Impunity, Vol. 8, No. 7 (B), September 1996. http://hrw.org/reports/1996/Haiti.htm

———. 2001. "Aristide's Return to Power in Haiti." Human Rights Watch Backgrounder, February 2001. http://www.hrw.org/campaigns/haiti/backgrounder.html.

Institut Haitien de Statistique et d'Informatique (IHSI). 2001. "l'Enquête sur les Conditions de Vie Haïti." (Haiti Living Conditions Survey [HLCS]).

———. 2003a. "l'Enquête sur les Conditions de Vie Haïti."

———. 2003b. "4eme Recensement Général de la Population et de L`Habitat–Résultats Préliminaires."

Institute for Fiscal Studies (IFS). Virtual Economy. http://www.bized.ac.uk/virtual/economy/policy/tools/government/gexpth2.htm.

Inter-American Commission on Human Rights (IACHR). 2004. Press Communiqué No. 19/04. www.cidh.org/Communicados/English/2004/19.04.htm.

International Crisis Group (ICG). 2004. "Une nouvelle chance pour Haïti?" Rapport Amérique Latine/Caraïbes No. 10. Port-au-Prince/Bruxelles. http://www.crisisgroup.org/home/index.cfm?id=2899&l=1.

———. 2005. "Can Haiti Hold Elections in 2005?" Latin America/Caribbean Briefing No. 8. Port au Prince / Brussels. http://www.crisisgroup.org/home/index.cfm?id=2899&l=1.

———. 2005. "Spoiling Security in Haiti." Latin America/Caribbean Report No. 13. Port-au-Prince/Bruxelles.

International Legal Assistance Consortium (ILAC). 2005. Haiti Report. http://www.ilac.se/sajt/bilder/pdf/HaitiReport.pdf.

International Monetary Fund (IMF). 2005. "Haiti–Selected Issues." Washington, D.C.

Jasmin, Jean-Claude. 2005. "The Emperor Has No Clothes. How Aristide & Co. plundered the Haitian Treasury; Dark clouds on the Alexandre-Latortue government. Commission d'Enquête Administrative." Ruminations of a Haitian Mofo. Posted July 29 at 12:03:00 PM. http://haitianmofo.blogspot.com/2005/07/emperor-has-no-clothes.html

Justesen, Michael. 2004. "Active Labour Market Measures in Denmark—A Duration Data Analysis with Immigrants in Focus." University of Aarhus.

Justesen, M., and D. Verner. 2006. "Haitian Youth at Risk." The World Bank, Washington, D.C. Processed.

Kaufmann, D., A. Kraay, and M. Mastruzzi. 2005. "Governance Matters IV: Governance Indicators for 1996–2004." http://www.worldbank.org/wbi/governance/pubs/govmatters4.html.

Kelly, Morgan. 2000. "Inequality and Crime." *The Review of Economics and Statistics* 82(4): 530–39.

Koenker, R., and Basset, G. Jr. 1978. "Regression Quantiles." *Econométrica* 46(1):33–50.

Kumar, Chetan. 2000. "Peacebuilding in Haiti." In Elizabeth M. Cousens, Chetan Kumar, and Karin Wermester, eds. *Peacebuilding as Politics: Cultivating Peace in Fragile Societies.* Boulder, Colo.: Lynne Rienner.

La Fondation heritage pour Haiti. 2003. "The State of Corruption in Haiti." Processed.

Lafontant, Joseph André. 2003. *Le mouvement syndical haïtien. De ses origines aux débuts du 21ème siècle.* San José, Costa Rica: Bureau International du Travail.

Laguerre, Michel S. 1994. "The Tontons Macoutes." In James Ridgeway, ed., *The Haiti Files—Decoding the Crisis.* Washington, D.C.: Essential Books / Azul Editions.

Lahav, Pnina. 1975. "The Chef de Section: Structure and Functions of Haiti's Basic Administrative Institution." In Sydney W. Mintz, ed., *Working Papers in Haitian Society and Culture, Antilles Research Program.* Occasional Papers No. 4.

Lamaute, Nathalie, Gilles Damais, and Willy Egset. 2005. "Gouvernance rurale et institutions locales en Haïti: Contraintes et opportunités pour le développement." Background paper prepared for "Développement rural en Haïti: diagnostic et axes d'intervention." The World Bank, Washington, D.C.

Lanjouw, J.O., and P. Lanjouw. 2001. "The Rural Nonfarm Sector: Issues and Evidence From Developing Countries." *Agricultural Economics* 24:1–23.

Lundahl, Mats. 1979. *Peasants and Poverty: A Study of Haiti.* London: Croom Helm.

———. 1983. *The Haitian Economy: Man, Land and Markets.* New York: St. Martin's Press.

Mankiw, N.G., D. Romer, and D.N. Weil. 1992. "A Contribution to the Empirics of Economic Growth." *Quarterly Journal of Economics* 107(2).

Médecines Sans Frontières. 2005. "Les soins de santé de base hors de portée pour la population rurale d'Haïti: exclusion et appauvrissement des vulnérables." Brussels.

Medicus Mundi International (MMI). Undated. Better health care by contracting not-for-profit, public serving, non-governmental health care institutions as an integral part of the health districts. www.medicusmundi.org.

Mendelson-Forman, Johanna. 2006. "Security Sector Reform in Haiti." *International Peacekeeping* 13(1):14–27.

MENJS, Direction de la Planification et de la Cooperation Externe. 2003. *Recensement Scolaire.* Government of Haiti.

Mills, A., S. Bennett, and S. Russell. 2001. *The challenge of health sector reform: What must governments do?* New York: St. Martin's Press.

Mills, A., R. Brugha, K. Hanson, and B. McPake. 2002. "Approaches for improving service delivery in the non state sector: what is the evidence on what works, where and why?" Paper prepared and presented at the *Making Services Work for the Poor, World Development Report 2004* workshop, Eynsham Hall Oxfordshire, UK.

Mincer, J. 1974. *Schooling, Experience and Earnings.* NBER Working Paper, New York.

Moran, D., and R. Batley. 2004. "Literature review of non state provision of basic services." DFID desk based research commissioned via the Governance Resource Centre, University of Birmingham, UK www.bham.ac.uk.

Muggah, Robert. 2005. "Securing Haiti's Transition: Reviewing Human Insecurity and the Prospects for Disarmament, Demobilization and Reintegration." Geneva: Small Arms Survey. http://hei.unige.ch/sas/OPs/OP14B-Haiti-English.pdf

National Coalition for Haitian Rights (NCHR). 1998. "Can Haiti's Police Reforms Be Sustained?" http://www.nchr.org/hrp/archive/pol98.htm#Police%20Progress%20in%201997.

Nicholls, David. 1996. *From Dessalines to Duvalier. Race, Colour and National Independence in Haiti.* New Brunswick, N.J.: Rutgers University Press.

North, Douglass C. 1991. "Institutions." *Journal of Economic Perspectives* 5(1)97–112.

———. 1994. "Institutional Change: A Framework of Analysis." *Economic History* 9412001.

O'Neill, William. 1995. "Judicial Reform in Haiti." National Coalition for Haitian Rights (NCHR). http://www.nchr.org/hrp/jud_reform_eng.htm.

Organization of American States (OAS). 2001. "Report of the Commission of Inquiry Into the Events of December 17." OAS/Ser.G-CPp/INF.4702/02 (accessed July 1, 2002).

———. 2003. "Second Report of the Secretary-General to the Permanent Council of the OAS on the implementation of Resolution 822 for the period between November 4, 2002 and January 4 2003." OAS/Ser/G/CP/DOC.3683/03 (accessed January 22, 2003).

Pedersen, Jon, and Kathryn Lockwood. 2001. "Determination of a Poverty Line for Haiti." FAFO.

RNDDH (The Haitian National Human Rights Defense Network). 2005. http://www.rnddh.org.

Razafimandimby, L. 2006. "Improved Access of the Poor to Social Services in Haiti: The Role of the World Bank." Annex to the Haiti Social Protection Policy Brief, The World Bank, Washington, D.C.

Refugees International (RI). 2005. "Haiti: UN Civilian Police Require Executive Authority." http://www.refugeesinternational.org/content/article/detail/5383

Republic of Haiti. 2003. "Plan-Programme de Developpement de la Zone Metropolitaine de Port au Prince."

Republic of Haiti, Interim Cooperation Framework: Summary Report, July 2004 http://haiticci.undg.org/uploads/ReportVersion8%20Eng%20FINAL%20Low%20Res.pdf.

Rotberg, Robert. 2003. *State Failure and State Weakness in a Time of Terror.* World Peace Foundation.

Salmi, Jamil. 1998. "Equity and quality in private education—The Haitian paradox." Human Development Department, LCSHD Paper Series no. 18, The World Bank, Washington, D.C.

Schneider, Mark. 2005. "Without greater UN help, Haiti will soon collapse." *International Herald Tribune*, June 24.

Severe, Patrice, and others. 2005. "Antiretroviral Therapy in a Thousand Patients with AIDS in Haiti." *The New England Journal of Medicine* 353(22)2325–34.

Stromsen, Janice M., and Trincellito, Joseph. 2003. "Building the Haitian National Police: A Retrospective and Prospective View." Haiti Papers No. 6, accessed at http://www.trinitydc.edu/academics/depts/Interdisc/International/PDF%20files/HNP.final.pdf.

Todaro, Michael P. 1969. "A Model of Labour Migration and Urban Unemployment in Less Developed Countries." *American Economic Review* 59:138–48.

Tremblay, Philippe. 2004. "Haiti: A Bitter Bicentennial, Montreal: Rights and Democracy." http://www.ichrdd.ca/site/_PDF/publications/americas/haiti_en.pdf.

Trouillot, Michel-Rolph. 1990. "Haiti, State Against Nation: The Origins and Legacy of Duvalierism." New York: Monthly Review Press.

UNAIDS. 2000. "Condom Social Marketing: Selected Case Studies." Geneva, Switzerland.

United Nations Children's Fund (UNICEF). 2000. Database.

———. Stabilization Mission in Haiti (UNSMIH) 1996–1997 and UNTMIH 1997. For more information. http://www.un.org/Depts/dpko/missions/MINUSTAH.

United Nations Development Programme (UNDP). 2002. "La Situation _conomique et Sociale D`Haiti en 2002."

———. 2003. "Outcome Evaluation: Rule of Law, Justice and Human Rights." Processed.

U.N. Secretary General. 1999. Report on the United Nationals Civilian Police Mission in Haiti, May 19, 1999, S/1999/579.

———. 2004. Report on Haiti. April.

———. 2005. Report on the United Nations Stabilization Mission in Haiti, May 13, (S/2005/313).

U.N. Security Council Resolution 867, September 22, 1993, (S/RES/867).

U.N. Nations Security Council Resolution 1542, April 30, 2004 (S/RES/1542).

U.N. Security Council Resolution 1608, June 22, 2005 (S/RES/1608).

U.N. Special Rapporteur. 2000. "Violence Against Women in Haiti."

U.S. Department of State. 2004. "Haiti Country Report on Human Rights Practices." http://www.state.gov/g/drl/rls/hrrpt/2004/41764.htm.

Vallings, Clare, and Magüi Moreno-Torres. 2005. "Drivers of Fragility: What Makes States Fragile." PRDE Working Paper, www.DFID.gov.uk.

Vera Institute of Justice. 2002. "Prolonged Pretrial Detention in Haiti."

Verner, Dorte. 2004. "Rural Poverty in Mexico during 1992–2002." The World Bank, Washington, D.C. Processed.

———. 2005. "Making Poor Haitians Count. Labor Markets and Poverty in Rural and Urban Haiti." Background paper prepared for "Développement rural en Haïti: diagnostic et axes d'intervention." The World Bank, Washington, D.C.

———. 2005. "Rural Poverty and Labor Markets Argentina." The World Bank, Washington, D.C. Processed.

World Bank. 1997. *The State in a Changing World. World Development Report 1997.* Washington, D.C.

———. 1998. "Haiti: The Challenges of Poverty Reduction." Report No. 17242-HA.

———. 2002. "Haiti Country Assistance Evaluation." Operations Evaluation Department, Report No. 23637, Washington, D.C. http://lnweb18.worldbank.org/oed/oeddoclib. nsf/DocUNIDViewForJavaSearch/718D6FBC34815E5685256B7A007F32F0/$file/ haiti_cae.pdf

———. 2003. *Caribbean Youth Development.* A World Bank Country Study. Washington, D.C.

———. 2004. *World Development Indicators 2004.* Washington, D.C.

———. 2006. "Haiti Country Economic Memorandum." Forthcoming.

IBRD 33417R

HAITI

- o SELECTED CITIES AND TOWNS
- ⊙ DEPARTMENT CAPITALS
- ✪ NATIONAL CAPITAL
- RIVERS
- MAIN ROADS
- RAILROADS
- DEPARTMENT BOUNDARIES
- INTERNATIONAL BOUNDARIES

This map was produced by the Map Design Unit of The World Bank. The boundaries, colors, denominations and any other information shown on this map do not imply, on the part of The World Bank Group, any judgment on the legal status of any territory, or any endorsement or acceptance of such boundaries.

ATLANTIC OCEAN

DOMINICAN REPUBLIC

Caribbean Sea

Windward Passage

Golfe de la Gonâve

HAITI

JANUARY 2006

20°N
19°N
18°N
73°W
72°W
74°W

To Monte Cristi
To Santiago
To San Juan
To Barahona
To Oviedo

Île de la Tortue
Palmiste
Port-de-Paix
Môle St.-Nicolas
Baie de Henne
Gros-Morne
Les Trois
Cap-Haïtien
Limbé
Ennery
Gonaïves
Grande Rivière du Nord
Fort-Liberté
Ferrier
Trou-du-Nord
Saint-Raphaël
Saint Michel de l'Attalaye
Guayampuo
Maïssade
Hinche
Lac de Péligre
Mirebalais
Artibonite
Verrettes
Anse-à-Galets
La Cayenne
Île de la Gonâve
Pointe-à-Raquette
Croix des Bouquets
PORT-AU-PRINCE
Léogâne
Étang Saumâtre
Lago Enriquillo
Chaîne de la Selle (2680 m)
Belle-Anse
Thiotte
Jacmel
Marigot
Petit-Goâve
Côtes-de-fer
Miragoâne
Vieux Bourg d'Aquin
Les Cayes
Île à Vache
Grande Cayemite
Jérémie
Roseaux
Anse d'Hainault
Les Anglais
Camp-Perrin
Port-Salut

NORD
NORD-EST
NORD-OUEST
CENTRE
ARTIBONITE
Central Plateau
OUEST
SUD-EST
NIPPES
SUD
GRANDE ANSE
Massif de la Hotte

Scale:
0 10 20 30 40 Kilometers
0 10 20 30 Miles

Eco-Audit

Environmental Benefits Statement

The World Bank is committed to preserving Endangered Forests and natural resources. We print World Bank Working Papers and Country Studies on 100 percent postconsumer recycled paper, processed chlorine free. The World Bank has formally agreed to follow the recommended standards for paper usage set by Green Press Initiative—a nonprofit program supporting publishers in using fiber that is not sourced from Endangered Forests. For more information, visit www.greenpressinitiative.org.

In 2006, the printing of these books on recycled paper saved the following:

Trees*	Solid Waste	Water	Net Greenhouse Gases	Total Energy
203	9,544	73,944	17,498	141 mil.
'40' in height and 6–8" in diameter	Pounds	Gallons	Pounds Co₂ Equivalent	BTUs

CPSIA information can be obtained at www.ICGtesting.com
Printed in the USA
LVOW010502051212

310153LV00001B/1/P